Masters' Guide to Love, Relationship & Soul Mates

Channeled by Mataare

Compiled and Edited by Carolyn Hawkins

Mountain Cat Productions ♦ Santa Barbara, CA

Masters' Guide to
Love, Relationship & Soul Mates

Channeled by Mataare

Compiled and Edited by Carolyn Hawkins

Published by:
Mountain Cat Productions
Santa Barbara, CA
805.895.4375
www.MountainCatProductions.com
www.Mataare.com
www.WhiteHawkReadings.com

Cover design: Carolyn Hawkins

ISBN, print ed. # 0-9755546-2-X
First Printing 2009

Library of Congress Cataloging-in-Publication Data
Author, Book Title, Book Subtitle/ - 1st ed. #2009912402

Table of Contents

About Mataare

During the past 25 years, Mataare, working as a clairvoyant, tarot reader, numerologist and trance channel, has traveled extensively throughout North America sharing his extraordinary gifts in seminars, classes and private readings.

Mataare, formerly named Paul Norris McClain, has been a professional trance channel since 1982. He specializes in channeling his client's own personal Spirit Guides as well as some of the most beloved and well-remembered Master teachers. Each Guide has his or her own powerful, distinguishable character filled with information and love for the client. Clients are able to make significant personal connections with all of their Guides in Spirit and are able to experience them as the available, supportive friends they are.

On September 20, 1992, Mataare experienced a powerfully transforming meditation resulting in a major shift in his awareness. He believes the personality of Paul McClain shifted into his greater soul self, whose name is Xiota-Lahmpsa Mataare. He now experiences life as Mataare, which he uses as his name. Mataare believes strongly that anyone can learn to develop psychically and spiritually, and offers courses that put others in touch with their own greater abilities and higher awareness.

About Carolyn Hawkins

For over 30 years Carolyn (known to many as Whitehawk) has provided simple, practical answers about life, love and spirituality through private psychic/tarot readings for individuals from all walks of life. Carolyn is privileged to be serving a private ongoing intensive apprenticeship with the Native American Chief, Sun Bear. Under Chief Sun Bear's tutelage Carolyn has finely honed her natural psychic gifts, allowing a deeply intimate contact with Spirit. It is through purity of intent, empathy and insistence upon clarity that Carolyn is able to facilitate the seeker to receive personal and practical answers from their own spirit guides.

Introduction

The beauty about love is that it is like a great mystery. Love holds something you never expect to occur, and feeds you richly if you choose it. For those who choose not to love, their reasons are always very reasonable. They make a reasonable choice not to love. It usually has to do with protection, separation or something of that nature where you feel you need to disconnect from your partner. Therefore, it is always reasonable. However, to love is a choice, and to not love is also a choice.

– Sun Bear

Partnership is one of the greatest difficulties people have during the course of their lives due to the confusion about ego, one's self-created identity, and one's true identity. Romantic relationships in this society have the proclivity to lead toward marriage and perhaps children. A form of romantic relationship between a man and a woman that does not lead to marriage is considered somehow to be not as good, a main idea that your society holds dear. To the point that idea is held as dear, many people base their identity upon whether or not they can have such a relationship. That is to say, if one has a successful relationship of that order, then one feels a certain satisfaction with their life. If one does not have that, then one tends to feel that something is wrong with their life.

Many claim a group identity or group ego. Therefore, many have tried to fulfill just these things, expecting that shall lead them to the fulfillment they desire. They are disappointed upon creating such a thing to find that there is still an inner restlessness, an upset, and lack of fulfillment, due more often than not to the fact that one has a marriage relationship and/or children.

Ideas of relationship have been thought through much more in your day than in days gone by. People are questioning many things about what has always been accepted and what has provided fulfillment, such as marriage. As a result, more marriages and relationships have dissolved in unparalleled proportions than at any other time throughout history. In addition, new styles of relationships and new ways of carrying on life are being cultivated.

People are learning that they can have more than one marriage during the course of their life. They are learning how to negotiate successful relationships with children of stepparents and extended families that often occur as a result. While there is much left to be desired in terms of where this shall all lead, the steps in the right direction are being made. - *Merlin*

The Guides

Azlo: an Eloha teacher

Cassandra: The Oracle of Delphi from the Goddess lineage

Chief Great White Eagle (Chief): a Native American Chief, part of the Sun Bear soul, and an incarnation of John the Beloved

Devorah: Romanian sisters and seers (Devorah, Helga & Olga, the sisters three)

Dr. Usui (Sensei) : Reiki Master

Enoch: Lord of Light

Francesco: St. Francis of Assisi, Italian Saint

Gaia: Greek supreme goddess of Earth

Great Bear: a Native American Chief, part of the Sun Bear soul

Helga: Romanian sisters and seers (Devorah, Helga & Olga, the sisters three)

Imhotep: Egyptian Priest to Djoser, architect of King Djoser's tomb at Saqqara, Egypt, mathematician. (Later incarnation as the biblical Joseph of the coat of many colors.)

Isis: from the Goddess lineage, Egyptian Queen, married to Osiris

Le Compte de Sainte Germaine (The Count): being of the seventh ray, the violet flame. (Later incarnation of Thoth)

Merlin: the title of the man named Ambrosius Merlinius, THE Merlin.

Miriam: Mother of Yeshua (the man later called Jesus)

Olga: Romanian sisters and seers (Devorah, Helga & Olga, the sisters three)

Philos: Keeper of the Akashic Records, who has never been incarnate in human form.

Quan Yin: Divine Mother aspect who is still living.

Sam Strong Body: a Native American Chief, part of the Sun Bear soul

Sun Bear: group soul of Native American Shamans. The man named Sun Bear, who died several years ago, has merged with the group soul.

Two Trees: a Native American Chief, part of the Sun Bear soul

Yeshua: ancient Hebrew name of the man the Romans later called Jesus

Merlin

Love that has no room for forgiveness is not love. It is a demon. It is tyrannical. People who have not room in themselves for self-forgiveness end up being tyrannical with themselves and others. Sooner or later they have to admit their tyranny and try to do just a little better. It is about progress, not perfection. Then one feels a little better and a little more deserving.

Azlo

In terms of connection to the Infinite, the expression of love is what is important. All true genius comes from the expression of love. When love is expressed in the form of service, it helps make other's lives easier to live and more pleasurable. In this way, the expression of love is true consciousness.

Sun Bear

All of your imperfections make you uniquely beautiful and unlike any other person. You are like a flower, where each flower is unique, even flowers of the same species. The little imperfections are your small character flaws that make you beautiful. This is why you need unconditional love, for the forgiveness of these flaws. You are not supposed to eradicate the flaws entirely. You are supposed to love unconditionally so that everybody can be who they are and be supported in that, but you need to stop demanding that others be what you think you need them to be. That is the tough part. That starts with principles based on love, trust, integrity, and forgiveness. These things do not have to be perfectly done, just used as guiding principles sufficient to get you through the doorway of love. Therefore, your imperfections can teach you about love.

Cassandra

The human form, in order to ascend its physical nature, must first completely fulfill its physical nature. That is to say, one cannot desire or aspire to one's ascendant body by seeking to negate the effect of one's physical nature, for the physical nature is also a product of one's higher nature. That higher nature knew what it was doing when it created a physical nature, and therefore that physical nature must first be fulfilled. In order to fulfill one's physical nature and then one's ascendant nature, one must understand who they are as a spiritual being, and be in a practice that allows them the opportunity to express in more and more complete ways that which is their love to express.

If there were a guide you might use for completion of the ascension of the body into ascendant nature, it would be two laws that you must follow completely without flaw. One is to know your self, and two is to be your self. This is so extraordinary that there is no reason you can come upon that can persuade you from these two things, for they are laws that are unalterable and all important for ascendancy. All who ascend the physical nature will, at some point, find this to be true. Most come to this by seeing that this is what is important and attempting to practice it, and also by having lessons in their life experience whereby they see more and more the reason why this must be done. There is no other way.

To ascend or to accelerate to the point of ascension of the physical body one must also have great courage and learn perfectly the meaning of detachment. There are many things from which one must detach if they are to ascend into their higher nature. The ultimate form of detachment is the supreme form of love, for this leads to the supreme understanding of love of self. This love leads to love of all forms of self, including the selves that seem to be outside of you.

The love for the self that is inside of your being becomes exactly the same as the love outside, meaning love of everyone else's being. Indeed, one more and more grows in respect, for not only other selves that are human, but also all forms of life and consciousness. This respect grows to the point that there is an ultimate respect for all consciousness, for one first has an ultimate respect for the self within that they have come to know.

Perfect detachment does not mean you sacrifice and give away all things to which you perceive yourself attached. That would be imperfect detachment and lead to sacrificial experiences that rend and tear the soul. Perfect detachment means that which is born of such supreme interest in higher truth that you come to find in the nature of your own being that all things first become less important. Eventually all other things do indeed become unimportant.

Perfect love can only be understood in the state of perfect love. No words can sufficiently describe it. No words that you might read can describe or instruct you sufficiently. No instructor, guide or teacher can relay to you every detail of what is necessary on the path, for the path is unique and individual. It is only the individual soul who knows when they are being true to themselves and knows whether they are dedicated to the laws of 'know thyself' and 'be thyself', and who has no other law but those two laws.

In those laws comes the supreme law, which is the unlimited law. All other words that might be said, while they may cause you to become aware of things, hold not to the absolute, for words are finite by definition and the absolute cannot be found in words. Rather that which is absolute can only be found by you in oneness with your absolute nature. It is there that the laws are written in ways that are irremovable and in ways that are ultimately free. You must recognize these things within your own being.

Also, know this. Your fears cause you to seek safety. The idea that you need seek safety is an insidious illusion, for that is to imply that you are not safe in your existence. To try to create safety in your existence, when in fact you are already safe, is an endless cycle of trying to prove something you never have to prove. Watch out and be careful for creating forms of safety that you imagine will be that which will secure, for security is an endless and fruitless search. Recognition within yourself that you are safe is the only security there is because of who you are. And who you are is an entity that knows itself as empowered and complete.

Safety and security does not come from what you do in the world, even though you will have many lessons of trying to create what you think is safe and secure. This in no way means that you are to abandon what you believe is creating your safety and security. If you too abruptly violate what you identify with as important, you will also create a rending and tearing of your mind. Instead, seek to move closer toward the understanding that you are safe and secure in this existence. Do not pay the terrible, terrible price for fear, believing in an illusion and paying the price of loss of your freedom.

It is important to be free and courageous above and beyond all other principles of the world. Without that, there can be no true love. Even the forms of love one does find, when one does not see oneself as ultimately free, are bonds and traps that limit the soul. Beware of the forms that say they are love and seek to protect you from yourself or seem to want to protect you from other things that they fear for you. These are not forms of love, but forms of need. The needs are usually not in your best interest, even though they may pretend to be.

It is important to know ultimate love and ultimate freedom. If that is not known, then seek it more and more. Lessons in detachment are learned therein. Forms of attachment grow strongest and tightest around issues of security and safety regarding what you think is enabling you to survive and be happy. These things are outside of self, outside of reality and outside of the truth. Detachment requires you learn to let go of all that entraps, even if it pretends to create security. Learn the meaning of be your self and know your self.

Sun Bear

At the age of twenty, a woman can innocently give everything she has to a man. At the age of fifty, a man can give everything to a woman. He has made every mistake imaginable, and, if he wants one, is ready to be present in a relationship. When men are climbing up in life, it is very difficult for women to be around them. However, after men get where they are going, their egos are a lot less pronounced. They are a lot more available to a woman.

The thing men will not do, from about the age of fifty and above, is become different from who they have become by age fifty. At fifty, what you see is what you get in a man. If you do not see what you like there in that man, it is not going to change later. If a woman wants attention, the best a man has to offer is fifty and above fifty. However, do not get in a man's way when he is trying to prove himself or you are going to have a very hard time.

Imhotep

Partnership is a problem and one of the greatest difficulties that people have during the course of their life. This is due to confusion about ego, which is one's created identity versus one's true identity.

In this society, partnerships have a sort of momentum or inclination toward romance, leading to marriage, and perhaps children. Any form of relationship between a man and a woman that is romantic is somehow not as good as that which leads to marriage is an idea that society holds as dear. To the point that idea is held, many people base their identity upon whether or not they can have such a relationship. That is to say, if one has a successful relationship of that order, one then feels a certain satisfaction with their life. If one does not have that, one then tends to feel that something is wrong with their life. This is a sort of group identity or group ego that is claimed by many.

Therefore, many have tried to fulfill just these sorts of things, expecting it shall lead them to the fulfillment of their desires. They are disappointed, upon creating such things, to find there is still an inner restlessness and upset, a lack of fulfillment in a great number of instances merely by the fact that one has a relationship that exists in marriage and/or children.

Marriage has been thought through much more in recent times than in days gone by because people now have more time for leisure. Previously there was only time for survival, and marriage was a very viable instrument of survival. However now, having had more time and more education for more people, women and men have been able to create a lifestyle with unparalleled levels of leisure never existing before in all of history and therefore time for pursuit of other things beyond mere survival. As a result, people are now questioning many things about what has always been accepted as that which is to provide fulfillment, even such things as marriage.

Many marriages and relationships are now dissolving in unparalleled proportions to any other time throughout all of history. New styles of relationships and new ways of carrying on life are being cultivated as a result. For example, people are learning that they can have, and that it is appropriate sometimes to have, more than one marriage during the course of their life. People are learning how to negotiate successful relationships with children of stepparents and extended families that often occur. While there is much left to be desired in terms of where this shall all lead, the steps in the right direction are being made.

Sun Bear

There is something very important about men, that women often overlook, that would be very helpful to women to know. The reason it is overlooked is that often men hide this thing very well. They hide it so well that sometimes men are not even aware of this thing or at least are not willing to admit it to a woman, and yet it is why men are compelled to have life partners. This thing is security. A man feels safe with a strong woman. Men may think they want someone weak to save and protect, but a man will never stay with such a woman. Secretly they want the security of a woman who will be there and who is mighty like their mother, if they had such a mother. It is a safety or a security issue.

Security is not necessarily an ideal reason for a man to seek a life partner, but what I am telling you is that women should know that men need security too. Men feel overwhelmingly secure with a woman being present and quietly strong.

In his heart a man needs to prove his strength to himself and to the woman he loves. A smart woman will let him do that. It is very important to a man because he wants to show a woman who he is. He wants to test himself for a woman, and this can be dangerous. Nevertheless, a man wants to do that, even if he does not know this.

Azlo

Never be jealous, particularly when you are in love with someone, for jealousy is the opposite of love. When you love someone, seek their happiness first and in all ways. To love is to seek the happiness of others and not your own happiness. Jealousy is the fear that someone else may make the person you love happier than you can make that person. It is the fear of losing the one you love.

If the person you love is attracted to another, be happy if the one you love is happy, even if his or her happiness is due to somebody else. Also, love the person who is bringing happiness to the one you love. That person has the same goal as you, which is to bring happiness to the one you love. If someone else makes the person you love happier than you do, be happy about it.

What is important is not that your beloved be happy because of you, but simply that they be happy, regardless of who makes them happy. Therefore, rejoice in the happiness of the one you love, if they are happy because of you or because of somebody else. Therein is the path of universal love.

Also, do not reject someone who wants to make you happy. By accepting that person, you make them happy. This is an act of love. Rejoice in the happiness of others so that they may rejoice in your happiness.

These principles of love and jealousy are not yet workable in your world, and yet these very thoughts will come into you when there is love and that love extends beyond you. This love is like the love in a family. Love in any great collective is also like this. If that collective extends as far as the world, then indeed the world is a loving place.

Sun Bear

I am going to give you some attributes by which you can recognize soul mate and the nature of God, either from the ethers or from a human being. These qualities must be present in order to have long-lived or even lifetime relationships with a soul mate. The first quality will seem like it is many qualities, but in fact it is the ability to see with your imagination, with your heart. If you closed your eyes right now, your partner would have to be possessed of these qualities, forgetting entirely their physical appearance, at least in terms of this first nature.

With your eyes closed, you would have to sense in your partner kindness, loyalty, insightfulness, devotion, and selflessness in the sense that they can be concerned with you above themselves at times. They would also have to posses the ability to care about themselves as an independent being, entirely apart from you. This is the first nature that your partner has to pass in order to fulfill the qualities of soul mate. That does not mean they have to demonstrate all of those qualities all of the time. They have to demonstrate those qualities at least some of the time. That is the first test.

The second quality is that they have to have the ability to learn. If they cannot learn, they will become intolerant, so they have to demonstrate the ability to grow. This may seem very simplistic, but there are people who have decided that they do not want to take in anymore. Therefore, your soul mate must have this quality.

The third quality is that they have to be able to demonstrate the ability to be just like you, not all of the time, but can they be tough like you can be tough at times? Are they fragile like you are fragile? Put them to these tests.

A fourth quality is that they have to able to overlook certain faults. They do not have to pretend those faults do not exist, but rather they have to be able to not let the faults matter at times. In fact, a great deal of the time they need to not be concerned so much with your faults even though they recognize them This is an important thing that they are willing to overlook your faults. If they cannot overlook your faults, you have a problem.

The fifth quality is also the key to God-consciousness and it is about your concept of God. Can your God overlook your faults? If not, you had better fire that God. Can your God demonstrate toughness and fragility? Can that God of yours learn or is that God stuck at some point? Can your God be kind, loyal, insightful, and devotional and care more about you and function as an independent being? This is a very important quality of both God and your partner. If they do not demonstrate this quality, it almost can never work as a permanent or long-term relationship.

Your partner has got to be more laid back than you. Not that they can be a bum or dysfunctional, but can they be somewhat more kicked back than you can at times? Can they take it easier than you? Can they relieve your stress by that? They have to help you grow toward being less stressed out. This is extremely important. Your God has to be able not to stress you out, being able to be at peace with itself.

Also very important, probably the most important thing, can your partner in some way make your life bigger. This is the most important thing about a physical partner. Can they make your life bigger? Of course, if your God cannot make your life bigger, more expanded, you had better fire that God because that is the wrong God for you.

The Great Spirit has to meet you at a certain point and so does your loving partner, so they have to have, at least at the beginning, similar values. This does not mean just enthusiasm and passion, but they have to have similar roots in some ways, whether psychological, religious or cultural. These roots could include philosophy or perhaps familial upbringing or the fact that you both want children. Maybe you both have the same spiritually ascendant aspirations. Whatever it is you have got to have similar values. You have at least to meet at that level. If you do not connect at that level first, you will not get past that level.

The next quality is can they be compassionate? Are they able to hear you, to listen to you? Particularly, if you are one of those people who are driven, can your partner/God hear you? Your God has to care about you and listen to you. If your God/partner does not fit these qualifications, you must redefine your God and your partner. If your God cannot receive you, you are in trouble. If your God/partner cannot be compassionate and listen to you, you have to fire that God and find the thing that represents sensitivity toward you, that which can hear you and not all of the time, but some of the time, can be compassionate, caring, and loving.

Who wants a God who is not compassionate, caring, and loving? What kind of God can expand upon you if there is no care? So many people think that a higher being cannot care about them because the higher being would relate differently to life than they relate to life. While that may be true, a higher being has the capacity to come down to your level, into your ditch so to speak, and relate to you where you are, bringing you forward from there. Therefore, your God has got to have compassion if you are a human being.

Next, the human being you are with, if you are seeking your soul mate, has to have some kind of inner life apart from you. It can be an inner similar to yours, but must be apart from yours. They have to draw or paint or meditate or do woodworking, something of an inner life apart from you. This is extremely important.

Your soul mate must be able to laugh and not take him or her self too seriously. They need to be able to interrupt an argument in the middle and make fun or joke or say that you need to talk later, not now. Either they have to be able to make fun of or laugh at themselves or stop a heated argument in mid-sentence from time to time. That is also what God does. God surprises you with unexpected pattern interrupts, its own patterns and your patterns.

Most importantly, a lover and a God must be a companion or a friend from time to time. You have to like them as a friend.

Finally, when your God or your partner hurts you they must be able to see that they have caused you hurt. They must be able to recognize when you are in pain. That is compassion. Furthermore, once they see your pain, they must be able to feel sorry that you are hurt because they do not want you to be in pain or to suffer.

God or your partner have got to be able to see that you are a human being, at least for now, and that human beings do not like suffering. Even though human beings may need to suffer at times, the Great Spirit and a partner must see when you are suffering and feel sorry that you are suffering. This is a form of compassion when they can show feelings for your pain. This is very important. These are the qualities of a soul mate and the qualities of God, which are one and the same.

Yeshua, Enoch, St. Germaine

There are those who love the truth, whatsoever form it takes, wherever it may lead, and whatsoever concepts and notions it causes to deteriorate. There are those who love the truth this much because they know the freedom and power truth can bring. That freedom is the power of love.

Azlo

Choose your partners freely. Marry if you wish. Reject any form of marriage or union that is as ownership of another person. It is difficult, but get past jealousies. Jealousy arises from children being raised in environments where they are not mutually desired by their parents and the parents are not mutually fulfilled. Do not look to each other for complete and exclusive fulfillment forever as if one owned the other. If you choose to live in that way, then choose that. Yet you must not base love upon narrow principles only or you will suffer again and again because of it. Do as you will, but these are vital keys.

Sun Bear, Chief Great White Eagle & Great Bear

The deepest most expansive love people can feel very often does not take place between people who are always together physically. But one of the most powerfully supporting loves that can take place between people in their physical expression does has to do with coming together, living together, and being together as physical intimates. Although this may not always reflect love at its highest expression, it will often reflect love at its most fundamental expression in terms of one's physical animal humanity.

Because the fundamental expression of love is connected with the animal humanity, many things first need to be understood about the human animal. First, in many cultures throughout the world women have traditionally had a different role than what is expressed in most western cultures today. However, this is not true of all so-called aboriginal nations. In many of them, including in most of the North and South American Indian Nations, women have traditionally had the role of the holders of great power and wisdom. Women were seen in this way because they are the ones who bring forward all life, meaning all men and women come through the woman. To this day women in these cultures hold a position of great respect and power, with the men holding the responsibility for the safety of the societies.

Wisdom, within the various cultures, most often was held by the grandmothers, older women no longer of childbearing years. The grandmothers most advised the Chiefs, and there could not be a Chief accepted as Chief without the approval of the grandmothers. However, women were not very often the Chief of the nations because of the nature of the different perimeter and boundaries established in area tribes, which may not always have been so peaceful. It was recognized that a man would lead other men into battle and help shape the men that were a part of the tribe. So oftentimes, the men were the Chiefs and the women held the wisdom.

Second, before speaking further about men and women we must speak a little about the nature of spirit. Briefly, every human being is in fact a collection of many, many particles of consciousness that band together to form an entity or a being. The particles come from the Monad, and certain forms of combinations of consciousness are called human and express what is called humanity. When this humanity spirit is born, it expresses as a human form, one form of it being through a human body.

Generally, the human spirit claims the body at the time of the first breath that a baby takes on its own when separated from the mother. The owner of the body, prior to separation from the mother's body and breathing on its own, truly is the mother. The spirit, that then claims the physical body of the infant, claims the body gradually over several years as the infant begins to become more an entity expressed as human through the body it has claimed in its own right.

The mother and child are virtually parts of each other until gradually the soul begins to more and more claim its being in the body. This is the reason spiritually that the mother and the child can often not psychically or emotionally separate one from the other. The child thinks it is a part of the mother and the mother feels the child is a part of her.

When that child lives its life, grows up and dies, the spirit or the essence of that being returns to the spirit realm. The essence can ultimately be reduced to particles that return to the ethers, not necessarily having any individual consciousness. Or that essence may not return to the ethers. The particles of consciousness that have embraced principles of consciousness that extend beyond the physical expression of the body can remain individuated to an extent and not return to the collective. The principles that must be embraced concern spiritual experiences, philosophical understandings, intellectual awareness, artistic expression, and things of this nature.

For beings whose entire existence was limited to a focus only in the physical dimension, one of two things can happen. They will return here to this physical dimension in some form and continue their lessons, because this is that with which they most identified. Alternatively, if they have not developed a sufficient ego and their awareness has been limited to the earth, their particles will subdivide and return into the Monad, gather with other particles that are complimentary, and seek incarnation. This next incarnation offers a more expansive opportunity for that entity to express. The particles could also divide into several entities that will then have a relationship to each other.

The souls with more expansive awareness who need to return to the earth for other human and earth-based lessons will also recombine with other particles. This is done in such a way as they will maintain a certain awareness of a previous existence in a part of what can be called their intuitive being. Upon incarnation, they will have a connection, in varying degrees, to something greater than their focus in the physical. These beings, formed of particles, also divide, subdivide and express through many particles, which may number into the hundreds of thousands, depending upon the expansiveness of their awareness and how much consciousness with which they can connect.

That is not to say that these particles that express in an individuated way express as one person's personality. What it might mean is that one individual is part of ten thousand people here upon the earth and therefore can identify with lots of other people. Meanwhile that one individual may have many particles, other than their current personality, combine in those physical expressions. There may be little bits of this person and that person and another person expressed through a single entity as well as through different entities, each with a different chairperson, so to speak, of that particular collection of particles.

In other words, one person may consist of thirty thousand particles of consciousness and another person may exist as the same thirty thousand particles of consciousness. However, one person is called by one name and the other person is called by another name. Essentially two beings are, in essence, the same being, just peering out of two separate sets of eyes. They are in fact only differentiated by the need to have a dominant consciousness, chairperson, called by one name or the other, who is the organizer of the collection of particles so as to learn different lessons. By the way, it is not important whether you believe this or not, but just try to appreciate the theory.

People who tend to find themselves collected in certain groups usually have a number of particles in common. Very often people who are attracted to similar music are attracted to it because they have many particles of consciousness in common. People in various cultural groups, people of certain political ideologies, of certain spiritual collectives, of certain artistic or scientific pursuits tend to share many particles in common with each other. They may not all be in entire agreement philosophically or in principle, but they are connected by the fact that they have particles in common.

Ultimately, all particles must come together harmoniously since they are all particles of the Great Spirit. The purpose of expression as individuated beings is to become edified and harmonious and to expand. In part, the infinite nature remains infinite by re-expression, combining, recombining, and transcending its nature through its particles.

All of this is also the reason why any single individual may feel divided within their being, because there are so many particles of consciousness with so many thoughts. This can cause people to have a difficult time knowing who they are or in figuring out their identity. The large number of particles combine in one person can also be the reason for schizophrenia or multiple personalities and things of this nature. These things are like the various particles of consciousness vying for dominance within the psyche and therefore there is an inharmonious collection of particles.

Soul mates and all other kinds of relationships come from the combining and recombining of particles of consciousness. The more life expressions these particles of consciousness have, the more connections will occur. Potentially a soul can feel like a part of everyone and everything. This is not the case for a person struggling with his or her own individuated identity. However, in the case where a person, for the most part, is evolving successfully, they increasingly feel a broader and deeper connection to all of humanity.

The reason that one feels closer to some people rather than others is the combining and recombining of particles of consciousness. There may be a greater amount of similar particles or shared experience particles in one soul over the shared experience of other particles in another soul.

One can also feel a compelling urge to connect to another group of particles in a way considered, in a sense, karmic. For example, one may have unfinished business with other elements of itself incarnated in another body. Yet those particles are in two different bodies instead of one because whatever job those individual collections of particles had to achieve on earth could not be achieved in one body. Maybe one collective of particles was in some way at odds with another collective and being in one body would have cause schizophrenia. Therefore, the particles separated into two collectives, but still they are not harmonious. They have to come together in separated bodies somehow to find peace and harmony. As a result, there is compelling karmic attraction, but also a repellant desire at the same time.

The ways of making peace with other soul particle collectives may be different than you expect. The fact that people are connected through soul particles does not necessarily mean they are going to have a perfect romantic relationship or that there should even be a relationship with the other person. For example, maybe the particles have subdivided in such a way that one group of particles is like a soul parent and the other is like a soul child. One ends up being a teacher to the other, so to speak. They are harmonious in their division as soul particles and their souls may be on a common journey together, yet if they were to try to be lovers there would be no fire between them. That is because there are lessons to be learned from the different combinations of particles of consciousness.

It is like this, souls are here for business, not romance. You can have romance. Romance is important. However, souls are here to do their business, which may not be convenient in any given societal structure. Hopefully, what will happen in cultures and societies is that the nature of the soul's business will increasingly guide the direction of the culture in harmony with the direction of the soul as human beings evolve to be able to embrace what the soul needs to express.

In western cultures, and all cultures around the world for that matter, there is a need to evolve the consciousness in many ways. Human beings are advancing philosophically and intellectually in leaps and bounds, and their cultures must evolve in order to embrace this evolution. This is a difficult transition for any civilization, and a failure to evolve will lead to the demise of the civilization.

One way the culture must evolve is to embrace more connections with regard to loving soul mates. There are various parts of this evolution that do not have to do with soul mates, which are things that have to do with advances in the arts and sciences and thing that have to advance in the area of politics and social groups. However, the nature of relationships seems to be unraveling in terms of marriage and families. Marriages thought to be for a lifetime, often end up in divorce. Sometime there are two and three marriages in the course of one lifetime, which can get confusing in terms of how to adjust parental relationships. Often a child may have a set of parents and stepparents and a third set of stepparents.

As women in your societies embrace and claim their power more and take their place in the mainstream of society instead of being pushed off to the side, men increasingly do not know how to relate to these empowered women. Men must learn to relate and women must learn how to embrace empowerment without feeling guilty or like they are frauds or fakes who should not be where they are and therefore self-sabotage. These are all parts of the required evolution.

Other matters of evolution would include the increasing embrace of multiple partner partnerships, homosexual relationships, and all kinds of relationships. Increasingly, the parents alone will not do childrearing, since the parents may sometimes be working. Eventually work will change utterly, but maybe not for a couple of hundred years. People who love children will raise children, not necessarily their parents.

How will nurture from non-parental people cause a change in the development of children no longer raised by their parents?

This certainly will immensely change society. What about when human beings learn how to create other human beings by genetic manipulation? How will that change your societies? This will cause people to have to sort through their ideas of what is perfect and imperfect. How will that effect society?

Society may not survive that reorganization, but if it does survive, this will lead to human beings understanding themselves in very different ways than human beings now understand themselves. For example, much of your psychology shaping your life is based on the principle that your first relationships are with your mother and father. However, what if your first relationship was not with your mother and father? What if there is no mother or father, just a genetic creation, what then? What kind of psychology would then evolve? What if you had two mothers instead of a mother and a father? What if you had two fathers? What if you have a group of eight people from two, three, or four marriages who raised the children, how would that shape your psychology?

Some people will try to keep society the way it is now, and will struggle and fail to do that or create wars, conflicts, and much strife. Other people are going to try to find ways to address and adapt to an evolving culture and society according to the nature of the soul.

What if so many relationships are monogamous because of the incredible power of envy, jealousy, possessiveness, and fear, which leads to things like murder, sabotage, and all kinds of dark expression? How many people are in relationships based on the fear of their inability to survive? That is, how many women and men look for situations that provide for their security, not love, versus those who look for love and forget their security?

Where you are going as individual spirits is all connected to the greater truth of who you are beyond the limited identification of self as a predominate experience at the level of the first, second, and third chakra. That means a change so dramatic and drastic that in the end you would not even know yourself. You would look back and not even know who the being is that you are now. That is how drastic the change is that is in front of you.

What does this have to do with physiological sexual, romantic, and spiritual relationship? What becomes important is that your relationships consciously support your soulful destinies rather than work counter to your soulful destinies.

Merlin

God's nature is love.

Azlo

Choose your partners freely, and be careful of the contracts you make with each other. You are human beings. You are free. Live with persons of your choice for only so long as you are happy with each other. When you no longer get on with each other, do not remain together because your union will become like hell. Union of two people is beautiful, but people grow and evolve. Two individuals may evolve in different ways and at different rates, meaning that sometimes unions are no longer possible. You must be free and continue to grow individually, and not spoil it with promises that will inhibit or not allow growth for both of you. This serves no one.

Sun Bear

There are seven primary chakras that are talked about, but in fact, there are eleven chakras closely associated with the physical body. These chakras can be called ruling centers or master chakras relative to the physical body, with many minor chakras. There are sixty-four chakras having to do with your humanity, most of which no human being on the earth is yet able to consciously develop.

In other words, there are a large number of chakras relative to human life, of which human beings are unconscious, unless they explore the realms of consciousness beyond the body relative to their functions here upon the earth. However, it is very difficult to explore those higher functions because humanity on this earth does not yet indulge in the higher functions.

Through meditation and through sexual relationships human beings begin to discover more about the part of their being that exists beyond their current understanding. When explored through the context of love, human beings start processing their higher functions at a level beyond the ordinary and enter into the extraordinary.

Vital doorways to the higher centers can be cut off through lack of understanding and misunderstanding, creating blocks that prevent a soul from accessing these higher centers. One kind of block is when a soul, not designed to be celibate, attempts to be celibate, such as in the case of monks. In humanity, those designed to be monks are relatively few, and they focus on entering in and out of the higher centers using other modalities such as meditation. Monks are aware of the blocks that can occur for them at the level of the sexual portals that could forever block them from reaching the higher levels. This is why they set aside the function of relationship to focus their energy and sublimate the natural organic connections to sex into higher functions.

Those who are not true monks must explore their sexuality. It is a rather unavoidable right of passage to your spiritual ascendancy with which you must deal at some point in your life or you will stop functioning spiritually. Otherwise, there are just not many choices by which one can activate, enter into, and successfully utilize these portals in the top of the head.

A simple physical orgasm is tremendously important to your higher spiritual function. Orgasms can be produced in any number of ways, but between sexual partners, it is essential that there are orgasms in order to transcend into a state of love at the points of higher consciousness. This does not mean orgasms must happen during intercourse or through other forms of sexual relations, but occur they must one way or another. Beings must make themselves available for that.

To say that love can stem from good sex is almost taboo in your society, but it is absolutely true. Yet you must seek something about love that is beyond the sexual aspect of the relationship. That is harder to do because many times people have many fears around relationship and sex. However, it is important because the body is integrated with the spirit to add elements to your life. To be disharmonious with your body is to make you disharmonious with your spirit.

Sun Bear, Great Bear, Sam Strong Body & Chief Great White Eagle

Imagine, if you will, sitting across from your partner, naked, in the light, with your eyes open, looking at each other for an hour without closing your eyes or touching. Maybe make it shorter, twenty minutes, looking at each other's eyes and bodies and breathing much more deeply than you normally do. Can you imagine yourself sitting still for that? Can you imagine your partner sitting still for that? Can you imagine looking at each other's eyes without breaking for twenty minutes with a partner you have been with for a while? Could you sit still for that? Would they sit still for that?

How much self can you bring to bear? How many of your insecurities are you willing to face about your outer self, your body, and your inner self? How much love can you have for where you are and what you are right now? How much love and attention could your partner bring to bear for where you are right now? How much love and attention could your partner accept from you where they are right now? Can you imagine? Can you see why it may be difficult to experience orgasm, if you cannot bring your full self to bear or if they cannot bring their full self to bear?

Dr. Usui

More than anything else, your journey requires forgiveness. Without forgiveness, there can never be healing brought by love. With the healing brought by love, there is openness and trust in your heart. Trust, as a part of your nature, is essential for happiness, love, and the ability to see clearly so as not to be deluded. You can never dispense illusion as long as you are in this world. However, you must not be subject to delusion as a consequence of illusion. If you wish to be clear seeing, honest of heart, and honest of nature, then trust is essential.

Merlin

It is nearly impossible to love unconditionally in this world because certain things about human love are very much along the lines of love and hate. If you generally love someone, they have the power to cause hate to arise in you as well. Unconditional love is another matter altogether. You should not avoid conditional love because any form of love is important and certainly better than no love at all.

Sun Bear

Even though people generally have a natural and organic magnetic attraction for their partners, they are often thwarted by emotional and psychic needs in terms of long-term relationships. In other words, if certain vital needs are not met when people are growing up, then they will have an emotional orientation to address those needs. This orientation to meet unmet needs may project itself in balanced or unbalanced ways. The result is a thwarting of the ability to sense right relationship or lack of attraction to the right relationship that will be long-term.

One of the most common problems to occur is what we like to call the Adam and Eve syndrome. It goes back to early man and leads men and women into very primitively styled relationships that are outgrowths of parental needs. That means men use women to satisfy sexual needs and women use men, primarily through seduction, to meet worldly father needs such as security. This is one of the biggest traps for men and women. It is so overwhelmingly powerful that it is by far the most confusing syndrome in your culture that prevents people from seeing right long-term relationships. However, with the right awareness, it does not necessarily prevent a relationship from moving to a higher place.

For example, if two people get together based on the Adam and Eve syndrome, if they remain together, it will be one of two things. Sooner or later the sexual relationship ends and they begin to function on another level of cooperation, eventually finding love again. Alternatively, they may never find a full sexual relationship again with each other. Either way, at some point the sexual relationship ends because they are together based on using each other. Therefore, they are cut off from their higher spiritual functions when entering into the sexual relationship. Without that, there is a distinct lack of fulfillment, leading to lack of sexual interest. However, the partners may be bound to each other due to common philosophies, religion, spirituality or children and through that may find a different kind of love that is meaningful and satisfying to them. On the other hand, they remain together and the relationship perverts, twists, and malfunctions. That sickness is then passed on to the children, and the children must deal with it from generation to generation.

Yeshua, Enoch, St. Germaine

The day will come when all must go further than love, for love is the doorway that opens a soul to a fourth dimension of existence and beyond. You may not stay at the doorway to love anymore than you may stay at any other doorway. Love, the power that moves the good through the whole, is essential for beings who seek to embrace the whole. Beings who embrace the whole are lovers of the truth.

Sun Bear

If you want some love, give some love away. Help others with their needs and watch what happens. You can always give away something, and then you will get something abundantly in return.

Merlin

When you know that you are loved and cared for, there is power. If you cannot yet love yourself, sometimes others can love you until you can love yourself. This is a great power. Not everyone can receive the gift of love, but others are open and can receive love where they do not yet love themselves.

Sun Bear

Some of the work you are here on this earth to do is through relationship, which relates to cosmic consciousness and gives your life purpose. However, many times people opt out of intimate relationship with family or other loved one. This opting out is because the confrontation created by relationships can lead people to feel as though they cannot hold their sense of self in the presence of intimates or family.

Relationships also are thwarted by something that is key to human life here on this planet. It has to do with how your civilization has evolved and issues of security and growth. It also has to do with how the entire population of humanity, animal life, and some plant life can configure itself cooperatively so that there can be an advancement of humankind. What is this one thing?

Here on this planet there is a great deal of competitive evolution. Through competition for survival, most plant and animal forms manage to find a balance within the system. Human beings however, have not found that balance within the ecosystem of this world. For example, human beings have yet even to figure out what to do with their waste. All other plant and animal forms, in a sense, have figured that out. This means nuclear and other forms of toxic waste are killing human beings. The waste could be used as energy, and maybe there would be less fighting over energy, which is the power to sustain life.

The competitive battle has brought forward some good things as well as some bad things in human beings. One of the darkest things the battle has brought forward in humankind is envy, which is very difficult for human beings to manage at time, even for spiritual people. Envy is the desire to keep or hold or even horde, and includes possessiveness and jealousy.

Envy and jealousy are what caused your creators ultimately to decide that if human beings on this planet were to mate, they should consider monogamy. Without monogamy, human beings might well end up having all kinds of problems, including killing each other. In fact, it is true that when one's spouse dies, it very often is the other spouse who did it. Why? Most often, it relates to issues of control, jealousy or envy that remain unresolved from childhood and are carried forward into adult relationships.

On the other hand, the issues of envy and jealousy, insofar as relationships are concerned, are meant to be addressed through relationship. Therefore, when you are a child growing up in a family with brothers and sisters, there is an opportunity to love and be loved in a way that is expansive. That is to say that if you are fortunate, you have two parents. Each parent has to address their own feelings about whether the other parent loves a child more than they love a child. Alternatively, it may be that the child will bond to one parent more than the other parent or one parent more easily bonds with one child and not another child. One child may or may not identify themselves as a more special or less special child in the context of these situations. These things must be worked out. However, many times these relationships between siblings are never worked out.

Psychology recognizes the value of these issues and helps people at least to cope with, if not heal these matters. Yet these are psycho-emotional types of evaluations and treatments that lack a certain spiritual redress. Very rarely is there a spiritual evaluation. The psycho-emotional redress is good, but many times, there needs to be an even greater context to heal the problems. However, to a degree, these issues are worked out or not worked out psychologically.

People then get into relationship. Ultimately, most relationships, with the exception of a few cultural and religious beliefs, are worked out as monogamous relationships to protect the insecurities of each of the partners. If the relationship leads to having children, the children are given two different messages. One message is that all love is the same. The other message is that not all love is the same. These duel messages are really never resolved as your society continues to grow.

The lack of resolution to this double message can lead, at an expansive level, to different types of bonding identifications between tribes, cultures, and even nations. This means that entire nations can clash with each other based on matters of envy such as "I do not have as much as you," or jealousy "I have more than you and I do not want you to get any," or "I have only this much and you cannot have any."

Envy and jealousy, coupled with the competitive nature of the human spirit and the need for security, if left unresolved, can lead to the deterioration of entire civilizations through a context of exclusivity. Historically it has led to the end of many peoples and species throughout the universe.

Envy and jealousy also indirectly connects to another matter. Why are you here on the earth? What kind of school is the earth? What is your purpose? Essentially, you can do many things here, but the purpose of being on this earth is to do something good. Attempt to leave something more here than what was here when you came. That is it. If every human being does this, the collective contributions of all people will promote a great wealth of culture and societies.

Unfortunately, there is sometimes also another point of view held by some people. "Get as much as I can in every possible way that I can get it before someone else does." That attitude leads to the dark side. It is fear-based.

As long as fear is motivating people, those who do good find themselves also contending with the darkness because not everyone wants to grow at the same rate. Not everyone has to grow at the same rate. Therefore, good cannot be forced on other beings. Those doing good will often find themselves in the position of either defending the good they do or fighting against darkness so that it does not overcome the good. This is the fundamental level of mind within humankind until the culture evolves past this stage, which of course human beings of this earth have not.

Of late, in the development of earth human beings, there has been a new thought movement. Initiated globally by beings such as Yeshua, it did not come in strongly until the 1800's in European and western cultures. The new thought movement came out of England and Germany. It was about a kind of consciousness that did not fight, but instead radiated principles of goodness without evil, positive with no negative to fight. The idea was the principle wherein all things ultimately aim toward goodness. The entire metaphysical movement and all of its permutations came out of this principle. Certain sciences came from this movement as did people of great prominence in this mindset.

The new age movement continued to develop and grew over a hundred years. In the mid 1960's the youth of western culture began to adopt the ideas of peace and love, along with the principles promulgated in the 1800's by those like Gandhi and later by Martin Luther King. The ideas made some progress.

Yet it is not true that by having a pacifist mentality the human nature, with its competitive instinct driven by fears for its own security, can easily overcome its fears. Some people may intend to overcome this instinct, but then there are those who would take advantage of pacifists and simply overpower them. This leaves the pacifists in a position of no control unless they assert themselves differently and more actively and sometimes, they may even have to fight.

For example, if you have an essentially pacifistic nature, how would you feel if suddenly there were people on your street taking over everything that was yours? This happens all over the world, maybe not overtly, but it does happen and has happened in places like South America, Africa, Russia, and Europe. What do you do with your fear nature under these circumstances?

The answer is that human beings on this earth require a certain evolution. The core of this evolution is through love. However, if love is protective, jealous, and envious, what kind of love can be taught? If love is not free, empowering, and supportive, how can it be the solution? This is a true challenge.

Most human civilizations do not succeed past the point of competitiveness. They fight each other to the death, which leads eventually to the end of the civilization. However, a few human civilizations do emerge from the dusty, complicated battles and survive their own errors of competitiveness. These civilizations try to help other struggling civilizations, such as your own, to evolve physically and spiritually.

There are great powers at work that support you on many levels. Nevertheless, at the level you must live your ordinary day-to-day life upon the earth you must have the ability to see clearly amidst the swirl of delusion. Even when you see clearly, that does not mean the delusion disappears or that you will not find value in the delusion, because you will. It is a little more complicated than that though.

How does all of this relate to relationship? If you are or were in a relationship, have you noticed that maybe your partner did not seem to be as awakened as you are? Why is that? What are you supposed to learn from that? Where are all of the awakened souls hanging out anyway?

Have you ever thought that at this stage of your civilization, when it comes to love, that relationships are often much more about work than they are about love? Even when you love someone, does it not almost immediately turn into some kind of work? The problem is then that most people would rather love and be loved than work at being together. It is as simple as that.

Another aspect of relationship is something we refer to as the Adam and Eve complex where the woman nurtures and the man protects and acquires. This means the woman looks for a daddy and a man looks for a mommy. The comfort they seek from each other replaces God for them. A man replaces God for a woman in the protection she seeks and a woman replaces God for a man in the nurture he seeks. This becomes extremely confusing. It is very difficult to extricate yourself from this syndrome in relationship.

I personally have spoken with women who say, "Oh no, that is not me. I do not need any man's protection. I do not need a man to take care of me." Then they turn around and say, "This man has no money. Look at his life. What kind of job does he have? He has no power in the world. I do not need a man like that." She thinks she is not looking for daddy. The men will say, "I am not looking for my mother. My mother is the last person I would want." Then they turn around and say, "My wife did not appreciate me. She was always mad. I was never enough. I just wanted to be told I did a good job." Can you see the Adam and Eve complex in these statements?

The things of which I speak are not bad things. However, when you cannot find your comfort in the Supreme, you have a problem. When you cannot find your protection in the Great Spirit, you have a problem. When you accept something way down the scale from the Supreme and expect it to fill your need, you have a job on your hands, because when you seek love in partnership you are going to be totally exposed. The big secret is that you really do want to be totally exposed. You want everything, you are not satisfied unless you get everything, and therefore you know you must be completely exposed to get it.

There is nothing wrong with wanting everything. It is a tall order for a human being to fulfill though. What eventually happens is that you learn to love unconditionally and you learn about acceptance. Therefore, when you find a partner to whom you are basically matched, you begin to learn how to really love them and really let yourself be loved. Surprisingly the work you will have to do is to let yourself be loved!

You might wonder why it is so difficult to let yourself be loved, but remember what I said about family relationships. Do you really believe your parents loved each of their children equally? Maybe your parents did not love you enough or maybe not at all. Maybe you did not get your needs met as a child. Maybe you are one of those who say your parents loved all of their children equally or at least that is what your parents told you. However, do you think in the minds of your parents, if you had siblings, that some of their children were not easier than other of the children and therefore got more attached to your parents?

There are preferences, no matter how much parents try to hide them. Even you love different people in different ways. But if you learned to love correctly, you learned to accept another human being whom you love on the basis of who they are, not the basis of what you expect or need them to be.

To accept someone on the basis of who they are you have to start with someone you believe you are capable of accepting. Eventually you will get to the point where, for one reason or another, you will not be able to stand your partner. That is when you pray, "Great Spirit, just like I prayed you bring me this woman, I pray you take her from me now." Oh yes, one day you are going to be making a prayer just like that. Either so you will choose to stay for life or you will not. Nevertheless, relationships are not what you think they are.

Love relationships are about learning to grow. It is work, and there is an unpleasantness about it at times. If you in any way think relationships do not involve a great deal of work, you are out of your mind. They are effortful and not only about love, but about growth even more than about love. If you are willing to grow in a relationship and do the work involved, then you can have a relationship. However, when the work comes up and one or the other of the partners is not available for the work, you will learn the meaning of loving and letting go, which is acceptance. There is no one who comes together in relationship and stays together in relationship who does not also accept the weaknesses and flaws in the other partner.

If you are looking for perfection in relationship, you cannot have it. The perfection you seek does not come from a partner in relationship, which at some point is a huge disappointment in every single relationship. You can have beauty, love, and ecstasy in relationship if you are prepared to do the work. If you are not prepared to do the work, then what you can have is a wonderful non-intimate relationship, which is what many people have. However, to have intimacy in your relationship requires work.

Another aspect of relationship is that they all begin and they also will all end, whether it ends in a lifetime or two or three or a half or a quarter. When the relationship ends, you have a powerful choice to make. The choice is if you are going to choose to love at an ending. What does that mean? How do you love at an ending? It is a nice idea, but how is it done? How can you compel yourself to love while still ending? You can because love is a choice.

Azlo

You are having trouble with relationships because you are doing them wrong. Until you live more as you were designed to live, you will not be capable of the right kinds of relationships that can truly fulfill you. However, the closer you come to living as you were intended to live in terms of relationships, the further you will come from your societies, which is difficult because your societies support you. Therefore, you must first make enlightened communities and enlightened people.

By enlightened communities, I mean educated people who are not stuck in the belief systems of their organizations and who are interested in learning, growing, and understanding more about the mind, the body, and the universe. I do not mean enlightened along the lines of people who practice mysticism because they will fail due to insufficient knowledge. Many of those who practice mysticism, while well intentioned and truly gifted, will not learn or attend schools and universities, not raise their levels of education and will not read anything other than mystical things. What good is that without the other kinds of knowledge? There are truly very gifted people there, but they must progress so that society can prosper. Seek to understand and solve the mysteries. Do not leave them mystical.

Sun Bear, Great Bear, Sam Strong Body & Chief Great White Eagle

Part of growth for a human being lies in the way human beings connect in loving relationships of all kinds. Many times people get together with intentions toward an intimate sexual romantic relationship, but in fact, the way their souls combine does not succeed as a romantic or sexual relationship. An example of this would be a soul parent, a being whose particles exist in and connect with many others throughout the world, comes together with a soul child, one who may be more parochial in their consciousness and not open, without so many connections. They could come together with the intention of romance and sex, but in fact, this may not be good for a long-term relationship because one is on a very different level than the other. While this may be good for a short-term relationship, often it does not work out for a longer-term relationship, because the relationship would be decidedly unequal.

There are also cases where people have a great deal in common, such as two artists, two musicians, or two doctors focused on the same journey, but they are really soul siblings, a soul brother and a soul sister. They have so much in common and are so harmonious, yet there may be no fire between them after a while. Initially, depending upon their needs and orientation, there may be some sexual energy or there might not be that much. This may work out for people in long-term relationships if they really do not seek to have a fire between them. Often though, they become like brother and sister with many sibling rivalries. Thus, there are times people get together with certain intentions and it may not work out according to their intentions because they are in fact not really soul mates per se.

Soul mates are souls integrated or connected to each other in a way that their souls are continually in a mating process, engaging in a kind of harmonious sexual union in the ethers, not necessarily through sexual organs. This is the equivalent of sex, and in fact, sex in the physical body is sometimes very incomplete if there is not also a communion in the ethers between those two persons. Soul mates have, amongst other things, the kind of connections that engage in an intimate and sexual union in a higher dimension, which sometimes also demonstrates in the physical plane. This can lead to, not only long-term relationships, but also lifetimes of connections over and over again.

As souls become older, they can develop a number of soul mates. One may feel mated with a number of people, which may not work out so easily if they are in a monogamous society. They may have serial relationships, one relationship after another or maybe have committed non-monogamous relationships such as multi-partners in collective marriages or unions, which have also existed throughout time.

In the Native cultures, there are ways to understand these particular different kinds of relationships as a part of our religious practice. Although most of the relationships in our religion fall into the category of monogamous, not all are in the form of monogamous relationships.

Merlin

Soul mate is something about which many people are concerned. What are soul mates? Who are soul mates? Where are soul mates? Many people also want to know how to keep soul mates, and some even want to know how to get rid of soul mates. Then there are those people who are curious about all of the various forms soul mate relationships can take.

First, there are many different kinds of soul relationships. There are soul siblings, persons oriented toward the same thing in the same direction, brothers and sisters on the path, who share soul aspects. In a way, all soul relationships are sharers of aspects, which is to say everybody comes from the same place. All of the soul substance of the universe as well as consciousness, and all energy, exists in a very compact, dense version until the creative urge comes upon it to create. All of the soul stuff in the universe, for the most part, comes from the origin of this universe, about seventeen billion or so years ago. Ever since that time all life forms and all consciousness has been changing, evolving, growing, shifting, becoming organized differently as life and consciousness unfold in this particular universe.

At this time, you are a collective of many particles of consciousness, whose energies connect in you. From our point of view, we see no difference between the energies of consciousness and the energies of physical self, except for the density. However, mass and matter is also consciousness, perhaps a different kind consciousness, but consciousness nonetheless. There is however, consciousness that serves a purpose to a human being at its level of function and consciousness that does not serve a purpose to a human being at its level of function. Nevertheless, all of it is still consciousness.

When you die a great part of your consciousness is left behind in your physical bodies. That left behind consciousness returns to the earth to produce minerals through waste that then again feeds the life processes. Every day you eat the residual consciousness of perhaps billions of years of earth and space history. As it is ingested into your body, you gain some level of awareness from that consciousness, usually impulses of one kind or another. Some people are unaware of the consciousness impulses from such things as food and some people are keenly aware of this. Insofar as food goes, you can attempt to design what kind of consciousness helps you stay in balance.

Not all consciousness recognizes it has consciousness. As an individual, you are not just a being of matter and mass, but also a being of consciousness that recognizes itself as conscious. The point where consciousness recognizes it has consciousness is the beginning of the journey of self-awareness.

For example, a wall is a conscious form of life, but is not aware of its own consciousness. It may become aware it is a conscious form of life if it were to become incorporated into some other life form and integrates its substance into the larger awareness. This is how things work on a physical and semi-physical level. Your consciousness works that way also. Once you become incorporated into some larger consciousness that is already aware of itself, you become aware.

The first time you became aware was when you were a part of a larger body of consciousness that incorporated you into its personhood, its identity, into its entity self. When you became sufficiently aware that you could be independent of that larger grouping of consciousness an impulse occurred within you that took you out of that larger grouping of consciousness. The impulses that occur are defined as your values, desires for manifestation of self, and expression of self. When these impulses became strong enough you sought expression in some form separate from the larger collective. This process has gone on and on forever.

You will also give birth to consciousness in a number of ways, one of which might be physical birth. That is, a consciousness comes through you. You influence that consciousness and your influence helps that consciousness to become aware. You also influence those whom you love. Those you love also help shape and design your consciousness. Teachers affect and influence any body of consciousness. We, of course, influence a great deal of consciousness. All of these influences cause your own awareness to become aware of things you had not been aware of previously in the form of new ideas, new aspect, and dimensions of thought and self, which blossom to a certain degree.

Some of these aspects of self that blossom throughout your life eventually develop a life of their own that may be able to integrate into your entire corporate consciousness. This means that your consciousness has different ideas, some of which work well together, some of which do not work well together. During the course of your life, you spend a lot of time trying to integrate all of your diverging beliefs, ideas, philosophies, and growth experiences, and learning how to embrace more expansive elements of consciousness that then reshape your spirit.

At certain points in time, you also let go of certain beliefs that are no longer a part of you. You may successfully wholly integrate yourself so that you recognize yourself to be an entity free from all manner of struggle and conflict. You also may find that you do not acknowledge and integrate aspect of yourself and are not in total satisfaction, but perhaps being at peace with different aspects of yourself that are not well integrated.

If you should die as a whole and integrated entity and choose then to return to this dimension and world for the purpose of further understanding and learning, then you would remember all of your so-called previous lives. But if your consciousness were to still be in some way fractured, but you were at peace with your different divergent aspects that were not yet integrated, then conceivably after your death you would move on and there would be a recalculation of those different groupings and aspects. If the aspects were sufficiently at peace with each other, they might seek another incarnation integrated together to create further balance. Some aspects might also choose to go on to some other dimension while some of the aspects would return to this world to continue on, in a way, combining and awaking compatible elements with the same intention as those remaining particles.

If you were to pass over while not successfully integrated, with diverging elements that are not only incompatible, but also incompatible enough not to remain in the same collective, then you are a complex person with many incongruities. If you were sufficiently upset with yourself because of the incongruities, there would be a recombining of elements of consciousness upon departure from this world. The incompatible elements would not be able to seek a re-entry, if they choose to re-enter, into this world as the same collective. They would seek to break apart into perhaps many different parts. These different particles, if at peace with themselves, would await further entry into the world, if that were what those parts needed to do.

The parts, which then seek re-entry into this world, would have different kinds of relationships with the other parts that were also seeking re-entry into this world. Those relationships would range anywhere from positive associations to negative associations. However, all of those associations will be related because they had been together in a functioning organism. Even though the functioning organism may have been dysfunctional to an extent, there is still a potent relationship of some kind between the divergent elements. The relationship is a result of sharing, not only ideas, but energies, which are ideas in waiting, principles and values, and there is a similar frequency or vibration, although perhaps with different compatibilities, different shaped ideas.

Some aspects may think they want nothing to do with other aspects because they may have felt trapped by other aspects when they were in the same corporate body. However, they still have a relationship with the other aspects, whether they like it or not. Because of that relationship, they tend to find themselves, upon re-entry into this world, around the same types of involvements and same kinds of people. In fact, they will even find themselves re-entering at roughly the same time period as to continue their relationship in different bodies, learning how to become whole, not as a singular unit as in the first grouping, but as multiple units.

The law of all existence, and therefore the destiny of all existence, is that all souls must eventually find harmonious integration with all other souls. This law exists because the greatest law is that of unconditional and unlimited love, which eventually is the only way all souls can accept all other souls. Therefore, all the little lessons you have in your life are ultimately to achieve that end of unconditional and unlimited love.

All life forms and consciousness able to find unconditional and unlimited love during the existence of any universe join as one of the creators and can bridge the gap between universes, creating universes for themselves. That is the direction of the evolution of consciousness. In other words, consciousness becomes another god. It exists in the universe as God, an entity of compassion, power, light, and love.

Where do soul mates fit in all of this? The particles of consciousness that move on to a different dimension and the remaining particles that come into this world still are connected, even though across a border. Yet, the border human beings assign as physical and non-physical life is arbitrary. Any aspect that has moved on is still connected to you, even though you are here, because it is a part of you. If other aspects have moved on in a successful manner, they will likely connect with a body of larger consciousness, awaiting the arrival of that particle at the point it is free from fear and ready to connect in some new way.

All of these ascended parts or aspects of your soul form your over soul. That is the first kind of soul mate, the relationship between you and the so-called over soul. Your past life experience, whether in this life or any other life, is in your over soul. That is how you get Guides. Your over soul, so to speak, may exist in the form of a singular entity or in the form of several entities, a collective of some kind that serves to assist you. There is the greatest intercourse between you and that over soul and it is the strongest, deepest kind of soul mate.

The aspects or particles that go onward may not unite in a holistic or positive sense in every instance. Some are guided by very unfortunate influences, but that is part of their growth. In addition, there are particles that go onward that are a part of you in a kind of limbo state, waiting to seek expression because they are not whole or strong enough to be part of anything. Because so much may have been fragmented from a soul, there really is not enough to form a soul and they become virtual particles of soul waiting to become soul. In other words, the particles are not yet mature enough to form anything.

The soul who fully integrates becomes a soul unto itself. If a soul of that kind comes into the world, they tend to be a master or an Avatar, for they are whole. One such Avatar is Yeshua. Another such soul is the Buddha. There are a number of souls like that who have wholly integrated, but still saw a mission in the world. They are soul mates with the whole world, which is why they feel the desire to save it.

In saving the world, they feel as though they are saving themselves. They are identified with the entirety of humankind and are quite empowered. It is because they are a part of everyone that so many human beings receive them. Those who do not receive such beings will receive them down through the ages because these beings have immortal souls. The level of their consciousness is such that it passes, not only to the people of the time, but is universal enough that it is true for all times.

Even though their consciousness may be fractured, a soul that is relatively balanced and at peace with the divergent elements in their consciousness can come into the world and form relationships of different kinds. They also have Guides, so to speak, who exist beyond this world. Those Guides are from where a soul has drawn its parts. The soul then in the world, if it comes in again as a whole entity, will tend to create a number of loving relationships of all kinds and tend to contact many persons and many forms of existence. It tends to have a sense of great desire and direction that serves as an impulse to keep the soul focused on what it is here to do.

It is also possible for such a soul to separate into particles, usually a few as opposed to many, and become what are called soul twins. Soul twins are those who do not fracture to any great degree and are at peace with each other, for the most part. A soul fracturing to a great degree might mean it splits into hundreds of souls. Fracturing to a lesser degree, as with soul twins, might be fifteen, twenty, thirty or perhaps even a hundred, but not into the hundreds.

Twin souls tend to function very well amongst each other. They function very well as soul sibling relationships, people gathered together for some particular purpose. Most artists are soul siblings. Musicians are soul siblings. Spiritual persons of a particular sect or direction are soul siblings. Soul siblings tend to have several soul families. For example, they may be a musician and as such, part of that soul family. They may be spiritual in terms of a specific sect and as such a part of that soul family.

If a twin soul occurs of the opposite sex, if they are heterosexual or same sex if they are homosexual, then there is a tremendous unbreakable bond of love between the two twin souls. This is because they were at peace with each other, even though they were different when they existed in one body. So that now they are two entities or more, they are still at peace with each other, even though they are two entities. Moreover, they love each other intensely because there is a tremendous desire to be spirits that intercourse at the level of soul. They are souls who need physical intercourse in order even to be alive because it is the desire of the soul to resolve all conflict. If conflict cannot be ended, the relationship will end and karma will cause it to resolve in some other form.

An example of how twin souls come into being is this. Perhaps a woman was born at a time when women were not allowed access to certain educational privileges. Perhaps she chose to have a family, which was also important. However, maybe she was always divided because she desired to study science. This desire was never met because it was an impossible desire to fulfill in the particular time. Nevertheless, this woman made peace about her desire because she got a great deal of satisfaction from her children, which she also wanted. Of those two aspects, both being equal, one was never resolved. Yet the two aspects were happy with the decision made to have children. That is an integrated soul.

If the two aspects had been unhappy with the decision, the soul would separate. If it were a violent disharmony, the woman would be sick, angry, frustrated, and things would be going wrong. The particles of both aspects would look for the day when they could separate. However, in this example, there was peace between the two aspects of self, and the result was soul twins. The particles were particles when they existed in one person's consciousness. After death, the particles separated and came in as separate people, incarnating around each other at the same time in order to create harmony. At least this is the intention, although it does not always succeed.

There are other types of soul twins. The soul twins we have spoken of have compatible differences. However, there are soul twins with incompatible differences. If there are compatible differences in aspects of a soul, the different aspects may choose to come back as a whole entity to fulfill itself at some time when it can fulfill the divergences. If the differences are incompatible, there may be a facture. The soul can do either one of these things. It is a choice because the soul has found enough love within its being to remain at peace. Peaceful entities tend to be able to connect with many other entities and connect with themselves harmoniously.

Soul twins usually love each other intensely because they have found peace. However, they conceivably can have fractured from each other enough to have some kind of conflict at some junctures. Remember that this is a simplistic way of speaking about twin souls, as though there were two singular whole entities. Nevertheless, those souls will eventually come to a point where they shall satisfy the need to be together in the sense of a physical relationship. This is because they will come to the point where they realize their love does not need to be restricted to space and time. They realize they are complete with each other, and they will move on, knowing they always have total access with each other. They know they love each other completely, but no longer feel the need to be together physically. The need simply disappears, for they become satisfied, no matter where they are. Whether they are in physical or non-physical forms, they have met their perfect union and they have completed. Such souls then are connected to each other for eternity.

It is a bit more complex when a soul fractures because they have incompatible aspects, incompatible dimensions, and incompatible energies. There are a number of reasons beyond articulation as to why a soul can fracture. There can be impulses not matured enough to formulate specific ideas or beliefs about why it can or cannot be together. It is just an impulse. These particles separate into the hundreds, and in some instances into the tens of thousands. These fractures can happen in other instances into the millions, depending on the level of severity of that incompatible construct.

When the fractured parts come into the world, they immediately become complex to exponential extensions. It becomes so fantastically diverse that even after just two incarnations, and sometimes even after just one incarnation, it is hard to track where all of the pieces went. Eventually such entities just claim their identity. They choose an identity from all of the places to which they connect and can relate, and they claim the consciousness that is appropriate for them according to the level of their understanding.

When there is a soul fracture, several kinds of soul mate style relationships can result. There are soul siblings, those with similar interests and direction. There are soul parent relationships, where a larger body of your collective remains together and the other fractured parts remain more separate.

When one being has the main collective of fractured parts, you will tend to gravitate to that main collective as a teacher or parent. On the other hand, if you happen to have a major part of a number of collectives, then those persons for whom you represent their soul parent will gravitate to you. This can happen in any number of ways such as a teacher whom you meet for a certain period in your life who can become a soul parent. Alternatively, you may be a teacher, which causes others to receive understandings from you. This is a soul parent to the soul child relationship.

Soul siblings often are found together in the presence of a soul parent. Then there are the official soul mates, those who are harmonious enough to have some sort of intercourse, which is not always a complete intercourse. It can be a spiritual intercourse, mental intercourse, emotional intercourse, physical intercourse or any combination of all of these.

You can see that even after two lifetimes, considering that each lifetime there may be hundreds of soul fractures, how easy it is to be connected with many other people. You may not necessarily be connected to others in such ways as you might want to spend your life together romantically, but certainly you can see how there would be a number of connections to many people on some level. The connections usually turn up as friends, associates, schoolmates, workmates, and everywhere because you are related to one another and tend to incarnate around the same kinds of interests. You therefore tend to meet each other.

The only reason why you would not meet some of your soul mates is that when you fractured you did not simply fracture into singular whole entities. You fractured and then drew to you, from the available pool, other particles of consciousness that you felt aligned with your interests, directions, and impulses. In that joining, you then connect with all of their relationships, the histories of that soul pool with whom you have joined. However, you can see that after relatively few incarnations the whole world begins to feel some rapport with some other part of the world. That is an impulse of love.

Those who exist as a collective may choose to allow some aspect of their collective to reign and dominate. That aspect of their collective may not have the interests of the whole at heart or it might. It may have the biggest part of the whole at heart or it may have its own interests at heart and not care about the whole at all. That presents a difficulty because, not only does that present a fractured consciousness, but also disease, dis-ease, within the consciousness.

The source of physical disease is the elements of your consciousness not at peace with each other, but that are instead at war. This happens because sometimes the souls that split gravitate toward each other in ways that are not always well advised. Some ways with which that is dealt is that as you get older in a physical incarnation you let go of certain aspects of yourself with which you are in too much conflict. You literally let go of an aspect of your spirit and change.

Therefore, you do not just become incorporate or discorporate at death. You do it all throughout your life, and those become the trauma experiences in the course of your life. You die and you change, incorporating consciousness all of the time while you are in a physical body. The natural and necessary process is that your consciousness is always linking, changing, connecting, refining, and transmuting, even while you are in the body. It is called growth.

Occasionally you cannot grow while incorporated in the particular collective you have created and chosen. In these instances, that is what creates feelings of depression and the desire to die and leave the world. The death urge comes from here, the desire to discorporate and find peace, believing you can cease existence. However, in fact, what is going on is that you want to reincorporate, incorporate differently in some way and have not been able to find a way to incorporate in the world around you. Hence the desire to escape the world, create a dis-corporation so that you can recombine.

This is where love comes in. When you have others reaching out to you and you reach out to others, remembering their love, it is because they were you at one time in some larger or smaller aspect. Their love helps you resolve your consciousness. It can be romantic love. It can be love that is of a teaching kind. It can be universal love. It does not matter from where the love comes because it is all other elements of yourself trying to help you resolve the discord within your collective, whether it seems to be outside of you or inside of you. Inside and outside is completely irrelevant because it is still two consciousnesses or more trying to resolve the disagreement in their consciousness. For some compassion comes from the attempt to resolve. They want to resolve other people's hurts because it is like a part of them existing inside of that other person or the other person existing inside of them.

Romantically oriented relationships occur when there is some sufficiently massive part in common between two or more persons and thus a desire to resolve their consciousness, which is in fact one consciousness. No matter how many bodies it is in, it is one collective working agreeably or disagreeably to resolve its issues, sometimes in the form of families or relationship or multiple relationships. Any way it occurs it is still consciousness that did exist as a whole trying to resolve its incompatible urges and differences. This is how you choose your relationships, families, and friends. The choice is all impulse, intelligent aspects of consciousness seeking to create and express love.

With regard to actual soul mates, who are they? Where are they? How do you create them? How do you keep them? How do you get rid of them?

First, there is so much combining and recombining, not only is it possible for you to have relationships with souls that broke off from your original part and recombine in some way, it in fact happens in such great number, particularly for old souls, that there are many soul mates of the romantic kind for everyone. There are not two or three, but perhaps tens of thousands of soul mates for very old souls.

A soul mates first impact upon you is how you know it is a soul mate. You recognize your soul mate instantaneously, no matter who they are, no matter what your state of affairs, no matter the age difference, no matter the sex. When you meet a soul mate, it is always instantaneous, unless you are in some form of great denial.

If you are denying being knowledgeable of yourself, then you will not likely recognize your impulses. You may only recognize the strongest of the impulses that pierce your denial or none at all. However, recognition of a soul mate occurs on many levels, emotionally, sexually, telepathically, mentally, intellectually, and spiritually. No matter whatever levels the recognition occur, it usually starts with one strong contact and then a realization that you feel connected on many different levels.

If you are looking for a soul mate, you will not be able to find one. You can only find a soul mate when you are not looking for one. That is not to say you will not have a vision of somebody you believe is right for you, but after your vision you have to let it go. To draw your soul mate you must successfully integrate and balance yourself or be on a path that leads to integration and balance. If you are not on that path, then all you can draw to you is another dimension of entity in some kind of equal level of disharmony as you.

If you look for soul mate, you are looking for something that will mirror where you are in a complimentary sense. That is to say, you look for a reaction to your needs, which is not who you are. If you are in a state of need of something that you want your partner to fulfill, you will not find your soul mate. You will find somebody who fulfills your needs at best. Once your needs are fulfilled, then you might be able to see who is your soul mate. But once your needs have been satisfied, suddenly the one before you will not seem like your soul mate at all. Your needs being satisfied may bring you a bit more into balance and you might be able to find your soul mate, but it is best if you do not look for them, because that is when it will come.

You could look for your need to be satisfied and not get it from your partner. If this is the case, then there are three options. You can negotiate successfully for the management of your mutual needs. You can negotiate unsuccessfully and remain together, leaving your needs and your relationship unresolved. Alternatively, you can negotiate unsuccessfully and part. Those are the only three options.

If your connection is not your most suitable soul mate, because they are a part of you, you can conceivably develop it into a soul mate styled relationship. Some people are successful at this and some people are not, but it can be done. It can only be done though if the individuals involved are not looking too much to each other for the satisfaction of their needs. If they are, it will never become a soul mate relationship, but will remain a partner-oriented relationship, a relationship oriented toward creating satisfaction through partnership.

Partner oriented relationships have a time limit, meaning they must go into soul mate relationships or the partnership will end. Partner oriented relationships are very useful for certain stages of your life. They can be helpful, pleasant, fulfilling in certain ways, but they will not last for the whole of your life in a functional way. It can be functional if it gravitates into a soul mate relationship, which means both people take responsibility for their own self-fulfillment, and then their negotiations become ones that lead to true love, true soul mate relationship instead of mutual co-dependency. If not successfully negotiated, the relationships are dysfunctional, training neediness into any children involved, creating an awful mess.

For example, partners who do not become soul mates and stay together have needs that go unfulfilled except by having the other person try to fulfill them. If the other person fulfills the needs for their partner, failing to take care of their own needs, then any children involved learn that is what relationship is about, getting somebody to do for you what you should do for yourself. The children learn that love is when somebody does what somebody else does not want to do for themselves, and that expectation then creates tremendous dysfunction. Most relationships in this world are like that at some point. Nevertheless, good changes can be made at that point, whether by 'do or die', kicking and screaming or in a very evolve kind of a fashion.

Most relationships that do not become soul mate relationships end, which is good, and is why most relationships you have end. They must end if they cannot become soul mate relationships. Why should they continue in a dysfunctional manner? Why should you remain in a relationship if it cannot gravitate into a soul mate relationship? It is excellent for non-soul mate relationships to end because it is an important stage of development necessary for your happiness.

Sometimes people hold onto non-soul mate relationships forever. This creates karma in their lives, especially when their soul mate appears and they cannot leave their non-soul mate relationship. What they end up learning about love is that it means some other set of principles than what true love really is, principles that may be equally of value to them, but create conditions that are karmic, challenging, and difficult and do not seem to resolve. Problems happen.

You can have many available romantic soul mates, not necessarily manifest in the exact same fashion. The love may be equal for all, but the way that love is expressed may be different. With one soul mate, the love may be sexual, while with another it may be intellectual. However, the love is very strong and the need to be in each other's presence or in communication and rapport with each other is very strong.

This is not to say that the best relationships to have are open or multiple relationships. Some are oriented toward having one and only one partner. People can be satisfied in a romantic soul mate relationship and create different formats of relationship with other soul mates as they choose. Some need to have sequential relationships with their soul mates, one partner for a few years and then another partner for a few years and so on. At best, these relationships complete, going on from each other in love, but no longer needing or desiring to be together. Each person knows that they will do anything they can to give access to the other person if they should need or want it. That is true love.

Then there are those who have no relationship with anybody in any kind of romantic or sexual sense, like St. Francis of Assisi. He needed no relationship. That was his orientation. Everyone was his soul mate, the universe, the animals. These types of people also exist.

Of course, there are also those who will form multiple relationships all at the same time. That can be hard, especially if there are children involved. However, if hard were the standard for what should and should not be done, then growth could never take place. That does not mean that things have to be hard in order for them to be good. It just means that if things are hard and it is important for them to happen, perhaps the easiest route possible can be researched and developed.

If the world goes in the direction of simultaneous multiple relationships, then this will be a much more complex situation for children. If the world does not go in this direction, then there will be generations of problems resulting from people wanting to keep the old standards. It may be best for some individuals to go in the direction of old standards, but life will go on in a new direction, whether or not everyone agrees with the changes. By they way, you will never get Homo sapiens to agree to one way of going about anything.

It is to the advantage of society, culture, and the individuals therein to research healthy ways of carrying on new developments in relationship rather than avoiding, because the changes are already beginning to happen. You can see this with the increase in divorces and multiple families. Rather than saying that is bad and it should not be that way, it is better to seek healthy ways for this to occur.

If it is continued to be judged as bad and not researched, cultivated, and developed, then society and the culture will utterly be destroyed by the lack of love in these situations. Therefore, human beings are forced at this time to explore and cultivate other ways of carrying on relationships than the traditional ways, not because the traditional way is bad, but because unless this happens, the world cannot go on successfully.

Whatever your orientation, single partner, serial relationship or multiple relationships at the same time, it can be a very simple thing. You just need to be certain what style of person you are, and that is what will make it a simple thing.

Remember, you cannot look for your soul mate. If you do, it gets too hard, and you will never find your soul mate. You must instead have the best sense you can have of what you want in a soul mate and work on yourself and your own personal growth. The more that you grow and empower yourself, the more that work will put you in the places your soul mates are located. You will not have to decide who your soul mates are because you will seemingly miraculously find yourself in partnership with the right person simply by the focus on your own growth.

By the way, soul mates are not perfect relationships, but they are a good deal better than any other kind of relationship. In fact, it is the only relationship really worth having and cultivating. No relationship is really worth having or cultivating, even a partner-oriented relationship, unless it is being cultivated to be a soul mate relationship. Otherwise, they are dysfunctional relationships at best. It is the natural tendency of all partner-oriented relationships to gravitate toward soul mate relationship, even if they do not succeed.

It may not be possible in every instance to shift into a soul mate relationship. However, the reason why all soul relationships gravitate toward soul mate relationships, even if not successfully, is because the urge for the power which is God is to create love everywhere in the best and the highest sense. Therefore, wherever there is anything you even think is love, even if it is a completely co-dependent and disastrous relationship, the force that is the

Creator will promote love, and love can grow even in those situations.

Learning and individual growth can take place in these situations, even if these relationships never get to the point of soul mate, and the learning and growth is really the point. However, after a time people begin to realize that the only relationship worth being in is one that is able to be a soul mate. This is because of the realization that the only worthwhile situations are ones that promote more love, harmony, and growth, and that no other persons are worth investing time and energy in on an intimate level.

Somehow, soul mates know they are soul mates from the very beginning, no matter what. They cannot fool each other. If people are together and they are not soul mates, they cannot get the words soul mate out of their mouths. Soul mates can also change their minds later, thinking they cannot really be soul mates with a particular person. This is not because they are not soul mates. It simply means they do not want to resolve their particular issues at that time, which is their choice. However, soul mates are soul mates, and they know it right away. Whether or not they ever intend to be together romantically, they still know they are soul mates right away.

Partner oriented relationship gravitates into soul mate relationship in the following way. When one or the other partner is not having their needs fulfilled, they first blame it on their partner. They might say the other partner is immature or not able to give what is needed in the relationship or that the other person does not know how to love. That is making it the other person's fault and they will then seek to negotiate getting their needs met. These negotiation may not happen nicely because there is blaming involved, but it might be the beginning of partner oriented relationships moving into soul mate relationships. They will fight without coming to resolution and stay together, fight without coming to resolution and part ways or fight, come to a resolution, and stay together.

The persons engaged in a partner-oriented relationship will usually let many things go that are not so important until things build up. Then when things build up sufficiently, they confront their partner and negotiate. It is a cycle. If these cycles occur relatively infrequently, perhaps once a year or so, this can very likely become a soul mate relationship. If these cycles occur every day, every week or every month, this bodes well for a short-term relationship that shall never become a soul mate relationship. It does depend upon how this is negotiated. There might be daily negotiation, but there may be love between the partners. There may be constant fighting, frustration, and anger, but it is still a constructive kind of relationship. It may also move to a place where the partners are negotiating all of the time and yet it is smooth, which is not a cycle.

Yeshua

Even though your heart may be filled with love that you are quick to give to someone else with your careful words, thoughts, and actions, there are times when you need such care yourself. There are times when your experiences in life require that you give more care to yourself. That is when it is important that you learn how to love yourself. What saves you in your time of need comes from what you have understood with regard to loving yourself. All of the love that you need is always here with you now.

Sun Bear

People come into relationship with needs based on their emotional history. It is very difficult to come to a relationship with zero expectation.

Isis, Miriam & Quan Yin

During the course of your journey, you will encounter hurt and pain. These things may, at times, beckon you to give up your love in favor of fear, self-doubt, self-protection and, worst of all, resentment. Be not seduced, and remember the truth.

We call to you and say, no matter what the hurt is that you encounter, no matter what the pain, endure further, for it shall pass. Consciously make an effort to relinquish resentment because resentment is your great enemy. Consciously make a choice to leave resentment behind you and enter into meditations with the Divine. Let your resentment be burned away in the heart of God. Never shall come the time while you are human that you will not encounter hurt and upset. Yet forgiveness requires your ultimate relinquishment of all resentment so that you may embrace a love that only begins at a fourth dimension.

Remember your life is about the business of forward movement so that your life here as a human being may be fulfilled and you may go further. Be aware of this greater context. Do not limit your development to your existence upon this earth. Rather you are a spirit in existence that is doing work, growth, and expressing here and now, and will express greater still. However, in order to do this you must face pains, hurts, and letting go, for only in this way can you transit and fulfill your human life here and elsewhere.

Merlin

Courage comes directly from love, love of who and what you are. This love can even come from another, because love in any form is very healing, and courage comes from that love.

Miriam, Isis and Gaia

You must live your life with character and power, with love and humility, and with the strength that shall increase with every moment of love, forgiveness, and letting go. Letting go is an act by which you allow yourself to receive so much love as then may come to you. This love will cause you to grow in power and become strong in the sovereign nature of self.

Sun Bear

Soul mates do not have to be sexual with each other. They already are matched to each other in a spiritual state as a result of cosmic union from other lives. Therefore soul mate relationships can exist outside and alongside of a primary romantic relationship.

Azlo

Instruct your children how to be sensual by loving and appreciating their own bodies, giving them no shame for any part of their bodies. Tell them how to use their bodies for pleasure. We do not mean instruction simply in sexual pleasure, although you should include this, but how every part of the body is to experience beauty and pleasure. Allow them to express their sensuality in all they do, in color and form, taste, touch, and smell. Teach your children to respect their bodies and the bodies of others. Teach them also to respect peace. Children have a natural instinct for sensuality, and it is often repressed. Teach them what is appropriate in your society, but at the same time do not make them ashamed.

Instead of teaching children that their body is a sensual instrument and everything about them is all right except their sensual organs, tell them their eyes, ears, taste, touch, smell, and environment is sensual. Make every part of their bodies a sensual and beautiful experience in an integrated way without the avoidance of sexuality as part of sensuality.

Miriam, Quan Yin and Isis

The chief obstacles to the embrace of love are fear-based anger and resentment. These things can close off the whole world of love to any soul unless there is intervention, and there is always intervention, which is the love of the Mother. In the movement of human beings within humanity there comes a time when human beings seek the embrace of the whole of their being in order to come to know a sovereign position. At this point human beings must grow away from Mother in order to know. This movement away from Mother is only as a child moves from a mother, but does not change the love between the child and the mother. Rather the mother supports the child to become the greater being, for which the child has been born.

In your experience of the world and the universe, you function within a vast context. This context is the Mother. Although the universe cannot fully be described in the context of Mother, Father or any gender-based expression, it can nevertheless be said that something moved within the Mother and created a previously unformed agenda. The thing that moved is love, a directed force that moves life forms and consciousness upward and expansively. Love is an organizing form, not based upon reason or need. It is a gift and therefore unconditional and unreasonable.

Human beings have many needs and are therefore confused about love, associating love with need fulfillment. That is not the same as love, for need fulfillment is quite reasonable, quite rational, and conditional. Not all human beings seek the freedom from association of love with need fulfillment. Such human beings are captured by the karma of pattern created by need and the fear that these needs cannot or will not be addressed. Therefore, they feel a need to control the avenues of redress of their needs. Such a force is quite compelling.

Why then should a human being ever seek to break such a pattern and find something else? What can be greater than the importance of one's needs and their redress? Only the revelation of the power of life itself, which is love, can reveal this to a being. Such revelation is enlightenment. When a human being is touched by the power of life itself and the pattern of fear is interrupted, even if only momentarily, that being has touched enlightenment. That enlightenment provides opportunity to attune to what exists beyond one's needs.

Great shock, change, hurt, and tragedy are often the profound awakeners. They provide interruption to one's patterns, whatever those patterns may be. Simultaneously the opportunity is provided amidst the shock, pain, and hurt to know something greater. If one chooses this knowing of something greater, then one has chosen love. Love for human beings therefore must eventually become a choice or enlightenment will fade away and again become the darkness.

Enlightenment is an opportunity provided by the Mother. When you are in the shelter of the Mother, you are safe. This does not provide sufficient opportunity in and of itself for a human being, without also a choice of love, to reach beyond and attune to what exists on the other side of fear-based needs, anger, and resentment.

The Mother and the Father and much, much more are now one. The nature of things eternal is such that it can be said the Mother and the Father have always been so. Such is the nature of things eternal, for all things finite are transmuted by what is infinite. The finite is transmuted toward the infinite in an unlimited manner, limited for human beings only by the choice to reach beyond or not. If a human being makes such a choice, human beings are accompanied by angelic beings, waiting on the perimeter for human beings whose choice is love. Angelic beings hover near to human beings. When the choice of love is made, many times it is experienced as freedom, peace, and delight. That is the presence of the angels.

Sun Bear

There are people in relationships who decide they want to have children because they think they need to have children, not because they should have children. These people become obsessed with that supposed need and structure their lives around it, slowing down their karmic growth because they no longer can see right from wrong.

Merlin

Fourth-dimensional consciousness, at least how human beings experience it, is tapped into by a consciousness of unconditional love. All forms of love that human beings touch upon are conditional at first because humans tend to be responsive to what addresses their needs or desires. However, when one has the experience of going beyond their limitations, capacities, boundaries, and restrictions in receptivity to energies, from within or without, that cause one to become more receptive then ordinarily they would be they experience a greater sense of well-being, inspiration, and health. They begin to see such things as hope, which is a vision from a higher level of consciousness.

If one is locked into three-dimensional awareness, it is difficult to have a sense of hope because three-dimensional awareness relies upon cognizance of data retrieved in three dimensions. If one has a broad enough scope of information and the ability to skillfully arrange that data, one might find that it points to a higher and greater order of things, thus coming to a stream of fourth-dimensional consciousness. Alternatively, one can become aware of creative tendencies as a consequence of becoming open to and exploring the creative realms of thinking and feeling such as dance, art, music or mathematics. These kinds of things open consciousness to something that cannot be defined within a context measurable by three dimensions.

Azlo

Fear exists because envy and jealousy exist. Envy and jealousy exist because you are human. Until everyone can have everything they want, you will always have envy. Organize yourselves, not so that the one sitting next to you can have everything she wants, but so that you both work for each of you to have everything you both want. It is not you for someone else. It is you for each other. You organize your society such that everyone is working in the way they love so that all can be fulfilled, not simply have their needs met. Working in this way requires great creativity and causes your genius to awaken.

Dr. Usui

Some would say that love for certain things is better than love for other thing, such as love for a human being is better than love for a dog or for a principle. Along with that, some would say a love for one's sense of the Infinite is nobler than any other kind of love. However, this is not so. All love is the same because all love takes place within your awareness or within your being. It does not matter if you love something that you think is expansive or something that you do not think is expansive, because no matter what you experience, love is still within your awareness. That is what is important.

This is how the Supreme operates within all existence, by getting into one's awareness in any way that they can experience love. Then that love blossoms within your awareness and spreads to other areas throughout your life. Therefore, anywhere within you that there is love there is also a doorway to greater and deeper love within your being. It is very important that where you experience an empowered state of love you cultivate it and allow it to blossom.

There are some things, which people think are love, that are not really love because they promote a disempowered state. Many times people experience different manifestations of relationship to some things or someone that leaves them less empowered. Although these things may help within the many emotional highs and lows, that is not love. Love is a power, not an emotion, and one is in the power of love when they are experiencing themselves as becoming empowered. Any emotion that produces a disempowered state, no matter how good it can make you feel emotionally, is not love. Love is that which empowers. That is the discernment between what love is and what it is not. Love empowers and emotions may or may not empower.

Sun Bear

It is very common for one partner in a relationship to get stuck, while the other partner is growing. You may desire and even think you need your partner to grow at a rate better suited to you, but really, it is not your business. You are not the one who decides someone else's rate of growth. You either have to accept that other person as they are or let them go. The inability to allow a person with whom you are in relationship to be where they are will otherwise thwart a very good relationship, making it bad.

Azlo

Do not leave conception to chance. Conceive only when you love deeply. If you desire fulfillment of the body, why think you must have a child simply because it is a natural outcome of sex? You do not need to have a child simply because you can have one. Have a child when you know it is right for you to have a child. To do anything other than that is wrong, and you will create harm.

Those who love to raise children should raise children. As your society increasingly allows those who love children to raise them, you will not need to think that simply because you can be an organic parent you should raise a child. When your society is more respecting, loving, and peaceful you will see those who love and raise children have a useful purpose in society. For now, a child should be for your mutual fulfillment. If one or the other does not wish the child, then consider that deeply.

Merlin

You will explore time and space in such ways as will baffle and amaze you. Amidst all of that you must come eventually to understand your sovereign nature amidst these tremendously complex and beautiful conditions. The key is love. What a beautiful thing love is, because it is so simple and easy to follow. The particular love you must follow is appreciation or acceptance of who you are right now. It is a kind of love that request of you to accept yourself as you are right now so that you may enter into a doorway beyond the understanding that you have claimed right now. However, if you reject anything about yourself, your conditions, anything at all, then you are rejecting an experience given to you for learning. That is why it is important to accept, embrace, and surrender to what your life is right now.

Sun Bear, Great Bear, Sam Strong Body & Chief Great White Eagle

Your soul mate, by the very nature of the fact that you are meant to function together intimately, will have the same calling to be in places and circumstances near to where you have a calling to be in places and circumstances. Therefore, your soul mate is likely to be right near you. The problem, if there is a problem, is that in order to meet your soul mate you must be on purpose in your life. If one or the other of you is off purpose in life, you cannot meet your soul mate. When you are on purpose in your life, the soul mate will be there.

There are several inhibitors in actually getting together with your soul mate. One such inhibitor is that you could meet your soul mate and they may be in another relationship already, which very often happens. If you meet a soul mate who is already in relationship, it is very likely the person they are in relationship with is also your soul mate, a harmonious vibration with your soul. Very often soul mates find ways of working things out if they are already in a relationship, because soul mates tend to stay connected with each other, even if they are already in relationship. They could become good friends or their families could become good friends, but there is usually good communion amongst them.

If one or the other of the soul mates is outside of their purpose, then that relationship they are already in cannot be harmonious with the true soul mate. In that instance the presence of the true soul mate is very challenging to the one who is in the wrong relationship. It is also very challenging to the soul mate who longs to be close to the soul mate that is in their purpose. However, soon or later the soul mates will be drawn together, whatever it takes.

Sun Bear

Relationships are not meant to provide you with happiness and meet all of your needs. Instead, relationships are instruments of growth. The longer term the relationship, the more challenges exist within them, but after the difficult period they become simple and easy. There is just a certain period where the relationship becomes difficult because the partners simply want what each of them wants. After they give that up, they find just how wonderfully they are matched, even though they could be very different from each other and not provide each other with all of the things they both want. What they become is a loving companion to each other, and that is a very, very beautiful thing.

Merlin

Anger is a step up from fear. A certain power comes from anger that enables a soul to act. It is not as efficient a use of energy as the power of love, but many times the nature of unconditional love is far beyond human understanding. Love is a perfect and powerful miracle that opens the soul to a truly wonderful experience of God. When a soul experiences true love, the nature of which is unconditional, a spiritual journey can begin to become conscious. Sooner or later the spiritual life must become real, not just a theory. For the spiritual life to become a reality means that at some point a soul recognizes that they want unity with the Spirit and they are willing to go to great lengths for that unity.

The closer one gets to facing the prospect of death, the more one must either grow trusting, loving, and faithful or fearful, dark, cold, and angry. If a soul goes toward faithfulness, it is because they have experienced love and have been healed, to an extent, by that love. They thusly are enabled to know the feeling of trust, which mends their wounds and pain. However, if the soul is unable to know such love, then there is a tendency to lose hope and contact with self and to grow afraid, hard, and untrusting. It can go one way or the other.

The love of which we speak is a long journey as human beings measure time, and is really a gift. One does not need to know anything other than the true nature of this love. They do not even need to know the true nature of self, but just the true nature of love. Yet if one goes far enough to know self and God, the infinite presence within their innermost nature upon which they can rely, then there is a beautiful journey with no need for anything further. And by the time a soul becomes old, having known such things as truth and having been called by the Divine nature within toward something greater, there must be something more than just theory and whistling in the dark.

Therefore, when you are angry, even though anger is like fear, but a step further away from it, something happens after you have been frustrated and angry for a long time, which is a sense of sadness or depression. That sadness is old, worn out anger. It is not useless, but just a sign that there has been frustration for a very long time and there is no more energy for it. It is at that point of recognition that love can be called upon for healing.

Sun Bear

You can choose a relationship based on any reason you want, whether it is for security, to be in control, to have power or any other reason. It is your right to choose whatever you want, and those kinds of relationships are available. In a roundabout way, these relationships are part of your spiritual development.

When you choose a relationship because you want true loving companionship, which is very special, you must position yourself to be loved. You must also position yourself to give love, which most people do not do the first or second or even the third time they choose because their other needs are too strong. Therefore, in your culture a person must just accept that they are probably going to make errors in choosing partners, as shown by the divorce rate. Thus, things like multiple partnerships are going to happen.

To choose relationship on the basis of loving companions, most people have to get rid of one theory, which is that you are a compilation of many parts. Merlin would say that it is balderdash for people to think they are a little bit of this and a little bit of that. It is total garbage thinking and has nothing to do with anything.

No matter how many parts you think compose you, you are still one being. You cannot possibly satisfy every single attribute and element of what you have defined yourself to be. That would be like saying you are thirsty and need water, but to get the water you must define every element down to the most infinitesimally small atomic structure to make sure you really get water. Not only must it be H^2O, but also you must check to see if in fact the atoms and electrons are properly positioned and rotating around in the precise manner they are meant to rotate. You must further investigate to make sure… If you do this, you will never drink the water. Stop analyzing and just drink the water.

You can treat yourself like a bunch of little tiny particles and try to satisfy every little thing. However, rest assured, trying to compensate for your biggest needs that you feel are unmet will cause you to choose wrongly in relationship. It is much better to go about it in a different way, such as you need love and you need to feel free to love. You need someone who you can see loves you. You need the ability to give your love freely. That is the simplicity of it.

If you give and receive love freely, all the other problems in your world will work themselves out. However, those needs that you have will raise their ugly heads and you are going to have to work it out. This does not mean those needs are going to be satisfied, but the primary need to love and be loved will be satisfied. All the rest is about acceptance of who your partner is just as they are. That is doable.

Sun Bear

I do not think that women understand men. If you are in a quandary about it, maybe you just did not know that in most cases many women are simply further ahead than the men they choose. This is not always the case, but seven and a half times out of ten, it is the case, and women, you are just going to have to get over it.

Men are likely to be more grounded than women are and that is perfect. Every woman wants a man who is more grounded than she is because that is how she feels the security and safety she wants. Not only that, but men become very powerfully beautiful as they get older.

You cannot really get hold of a man before fifty because he is not who he is before fifty. Men usually need to prove themselves against the world, whether they like it or not, and are busy trying to create their lives. After fifty, they begin to relax. After sixty, men begin to be present for women. That is why so many younger women look for older men. The man's ego is a little less strong because he has done most of what he wanted to do in the world and he is ready to pay some attention to a woman.

Also by fifty men are pretty much who they are going to be, and you cannot get them to change. What you see is what you get when a man is fifty or so. However, the thing you will see is that if there is true love and care, a man can really be there for a woman.

Between the ages of thirty-five and fifty men are very hard to get hold of for women. Men younger than thirty-five are very pliable, very active, and full of energy. By about thirty-five or so men need to do something in the world, and nobody better get in their way. In their forties men tend to be pretty negative, suspicious, and struggling. In most cases, they are just not available. After about fifty, men know themselves pretty well. That is pretty much the design of things.

Merlin

The mind is a tool given to a human being to use. It is not meant that you fight the mind or that you identify yourself with it, for in fact what you are is greater than the mind. However, an undisciplined mind can fuel many emotions, particularly anger, resentment, and frustration. An undisciplined mind tends to find fuel through impatience, which fuels ambitions intended to address your ego drives. Resentment is the thing that fuels such things as avarice, murder, fear, and doubt and is driven at the level of the mind when the soul becomes identified with emotion as self. The mind and the emotions are such powerful things that most people think they are some combination of their mind and their emotions.

Understand that if you are born into this world as a human being, you are a fleshy thing. As such, you are like the other animals around you, a human animal as it were. Even though you have certain potential that most animals do not have here on the earth, that potential can hardly be realized if you do not find what is human about you. That is, you must find the part of you that is soulful, the part of you that can respond to something other than your drives at the level of your ego.

You are soulful. However, you can only know that when the mind is still. When the mind is still, then you can apply the remedy of love and forgiveness, and the remedy of patience for resentment. In fact, patience really is the evidence of your faith. Faith is the product of being possessed of love. The by-product of love is truth and forgiveness.

Most people think the ego is something like pride, but pride really is simply one of the by-products of the ego, and there is nothing wrong with pride. A false pride can lead you in many untoward directions. The ego, as I speak of it, is the identity a person thinks they are because they become identified with their drive for security, prestige, sex, and security. Every animal, including the human animal, seeks to be secure in his or her person. Every animal seeks to have a measure of emotional security through whatever it is that gives that sense of security. As a human being, you have an instinctual drive within you to have security.

The sex drive is an instinct to propagate the species. It may have a pleasurable function as well and may be an expression of your affection, but the instinct is a drive to continue the species. Every animal wants to survive at the level of its species and therefore in human being this instinct arises at some point in time. If the sex drive is strong enough at any particular time, then it is present enough for one to become identified with it and preoccupied with it. In the case of most animals, including human animals, the instinct for sex and security, emotional and physical, instinctually preoccupies the mind.

Human beings are also social animals. Some human beings resent this fact and would rather love a dog, cat, lion, tiger, whale or whatever endangered species is around. Other humans resent animals and welcome only humans. Either way human beings have an instinctual need for social interaction because without it, independently it is very difficult to survive. This means your social instinct as a human animal drives you, preoccupies you with positioning yourself within your society in whatever way with which you instinctually identify that you believe serves your interest in survival. When the social instinct is out of control it drives untoward ambitions and makes a person care about such things as prestige because the greater the prestige, presumably, the greater positioning within society to negotiate survival.

The instinctual drives that occupy a human beings mind are the substance, the foundation of the ego, the identification you have as a consequence of the preoccupation of your mind and emotions. With these instinctual pulls, you create a sense of self, an identity, either positive or negative or a combination of both, and this is what you believe you are.

To discover who you are in truth you must become quiet enough within your own being. Within the inner stillness is wisdom that lies deep down within the innermost self, the powerful, quiet, and still voice that is greater than other things. That is not the mind. The mind is a tool. However, the undisciplined mind can get in the way of knowing who you are because it is the foundation of error. It is the foundation of what has been termed by some as sin, or missing the mark. This is why it is important to learn how to still your mind. Only then can you understand what it means to love, to forgive, and truly let go and let God.

Sun Bear

To make it simple, there are many different kinds of soul relationships. Soul siblings need to work together toward the same higher cause, and they have all kinds of sibling family issues to resolve. Soul mates need to function together intimately for a reason important to the growth of their souls. Soul parents need to guide soul children. Soul children need to learn from soul parents.

Soul twins need to resolve the issues that caused the split in their soul. They instantly recognize each other, see themselves in each other, and must help each other. There is not a way around helping each other because their souls split off from each other and they are incomplete without each other. When they have resolved their issues with each other, they must go back-to-back, like the two sides of a coin, which is then the perfect relationship.

Sun Bear

Relationships based on exclusivity are fear-based to protect against jealousy and envy. If you choose not to structure your relationship for protection from your fears and choose instead to expand your freedom, then you will get flack from your culture. Very few people in your culture are adequately prepared to live with this flack. They will not find it easy to live, even with their self, when they choose freedom over protection.

Azlo

Do not confuse your emotions with love. You have feelings, but many of your feelings are based on knowledge that is conscious, less conscious, and subconscious, which are all elements of your mind. These elements promote intuitions in your being that give you feelings. That is not love. It is intuition, one of your senses. It is not even your mind any more than your vision or your hearing is mind. Your intuition is a sense based upon knowledge of which you are not fully conscious that produces emotions in you. Emotions run rampant, unguided and do not produce keen intuitions. They have very little to do with love.

When I speak of heart I speak of what you know is love. Love must become a conscious decision at some point. You cannot love unless you chose to be more conscious of love than other things, because you will have to choose to be conscious in your love. When you make a conscious decision to love, then love flows, and your emotions will flow in harmony with such a decision.

You inherently know love, but will have to make decisions of mind based upon your will to love for greater love to flow through you. Love exists within you and is fundamental to your nature, but you must decide about love. It is not organic in its expression. It is organic in its initial presence, but in its development, you must make a decision to love. You must choose love or love cannot be. That is the message of all of the great teachers. You must dwell upon love. In order to do that you must forgive. That is different from any intellectual development, which you also must have or else there is no survival and there can then be no love.

When it comes to relationship, please consider this. How can you love and possess when any and every form of love that has ever lasted, whether with a lover, child or parent, has only lasted when you have let go of possessing it? It is only when you have let go that you have been able to love.

Marriage has been for survival. You do not need marriage for survival past the point when you are able better to organize your society. Then you can love without the need to base what you call love upon your fear that love will somehow escape you if your lovers escape you. If that is the case for you, then you do not know who you are. You must know who you are and believe in yourself, then you can marry for love.

If it fulfills you, have a lifetime mate. If it does not fulfill you, no longer have that mate. It is as simple as that. If you believe in a lifetime mate and must have a mate for a lifetime, it will fulfill you. However, it will grow harder and harder to find a lifetime mate because you may not need a mate to survive. Therefore, there is no need to be with one mate for a lifetime other than for love. If you truly love, you may not need that lover in the format of a lifetime mate.

Have you noticed that people who are together until the end of their lives, if they still love each other, and many of them do not, they have accepted each other as they are with all of their imperfections and love each other anyway? They have stopped trying to make their partner into who each needs the other to be. If they do not stop trying to make their partners over into who they need them to be, then they fight, but they still love each other. Somehow, their love supersedes their arguments, even if they love to compete or battle with each other. That is the form of relationship you are conditioned toward at this point.

However, you are getting so intelligent that you will supersede that conditioning because of your intellect in a very simple and common sense sort of way. When a woman does not need a man for money to survive, then she will need a man for sex, love, communication, creativity, and combine power. If you develop an institution based on those principles, you are well on your way to further development. The current paradigm for relationship is based upon possession of each other, and that will not work. You need a new paradigm for relationship.

The difficulty you will encounter is that many people, both women and men, cannot relinquish the old conditioning. It is very difficult to relinquish conditioning, even if you want to relinquish it. The only way to let it go is to have faith in a greater purpose and faith that you are a part of that greater purpose. Then you will start to see the greater purpose, and will fall into harmony with it. As you fall into harmony with the greater purpose you will find yourself amidst those who believe similarly, and you will have your emotional needs met. You must do this based on organizing your lives to make it easier for each other to have this work.

If you marry because it makes it easier for each of you to live, that is not love. It is helping each other, and maybe you will grow to love each other. Maybe you do not need to love each other. Maybe you will find a way to live with each other and help each other and love each other, but not necessarily be exclusive to each other if you choose not to be.

If being exclusive in relationship fulfills each of you, be exclusive. However, if you were exclusive beings, where is that one whom you have always loved? You have obviously left him or her. How exclusive can you have been? If you are with your partner now and you are exclusive, congratulations. You are one of the exclusive people and you should remain so. This exclusivity is something based upon your need because you need each other to live. That is being of service to each other, and that can be love.

However, when it comes to exclusivity love does not posses. It just does not posses. Other things possess, and these things may be important to you. If the other things are important to you and they fulfill you, you should have them because you should have whatever fulfills you. You must have whatever fulfills you in abundance in order to be human, provided you follow a few simple rules that will help you. These rules for you to follow have been left over and over again in all of the great teachings.

The truth is that you must expand your idea of love, not in any particular direction, but in a direction that can satisfy you in some other way that you do not yet know. You will come to know it and you will get what you want without trying to chase after it. That is how the mind works. First expand your idea of love, and then you make it what you want. You were not designed to be alone. What you do with your partners is something you will have to work out. Nevertheless, you were not designed to be alone.

Yeshua, Enoch, St. Germaine

Many love the light and move toward it. Many fear the darkness and avoid it. Infinity requires that you persist through both the light and the darkness and find what is greater than both the light and the darkness. The soul that shall see only the light does not see the truth anymore than the soul that persists only in the shadow. The light and the dark are both but aspect of something less than the whole, for what is the whole is greater than the light and the dark.

Sun Bear

All have heard that love means letting go. However, why would that be said when everybody wants to get and hold onto love? What then does it really mean? It means that love has to do with letting go of self-centered concerns, which is very difficult to comprehend. Love is about letting go of real and perceived needs.

Tremendous progress has been made in society regarding individualist pursuit of happiness, fulfillment, and freedom. Yet one can easily imagine how selfishness, one's self-interest, may often work counter to other people's concerns. The result is that one, consciously or unconsciously, steps on the toes of other people. Everyone wants freedom in his or her own way, which is fine, but one has to become very tolerant and conscious of others for that to work. Judgments of others must be given up and tolerance and awareness of others used in its place. Therefore, tolerance and consciousness are qualities that must go with this attitude of freedom.

How can one have consciousness of others when sometimes the interests of others are in conflict with one's own interests? This is such a difficult challenge that entire societies, entire worlds have difficulty getting beyond this, and they die out. Therefore, how does one get past conflict with others? The work takes place on an individual basis. Individuals must seek to create harmony in their lives and in terms of their interface with those who are around them, individual by individual. The greatest work is between oneself and their enemies, coming to terms with one's enemies and loving one's enemies. Entire dimensions are transformed into a higher plane of consciousness because many beings within that plane express a consciousness that is transformative and essentially, they create heavens out of earth, so to speak.

Azlo

You want there to be more love for everyone. However, when faced with those who impose their uncaring will upon you or within your environment, do you allow that? No, you do not. You are competitive. Otherwise, you would not care. You want your way to supersede the way of others. To what lengths are you willing to go in order for your way to win out? You are willing to go to any lengths to win. That is competition, not love.

Merlin

If you have struggles with your parents, you must forgive your parents and not hold resentment toward them, particularly your fathers. For women who want relationships, look deeply at your resentment toward your father. Let the resentment go and instead honor your father. Men and women, who want relationships but fear them, understand that although you may be alone, human beings are not designed to be alone. Sometimes you may be alone, but you are not designed this way. If you do not wish to be alone and you are, look at your anger and resentment, and look at your relationship to your parents. Make allowances for your parents and find forgiveness if you want love.

Sun Bear

Some people are married. Some people are single. Some people are in relationships. Some people are living with a partner. Some people are alone in terms of relationship. Some people may not have had a relationship in a long time, maybe never. However, in all of these circumstances there is a great challenge. That challenge is love. Only when there is sufficient love do you really know who you are. Only when you have sufficient love within your experience of life do you have a chance to see and feel yourself shine in that experience and go beyond what the world had otherwise been prior to that experience.

It is important to remember that what you are experiencing in love is really not the other person. You are experiencing love that is in your own being. The love does not come from the other person. Certainly, something must come from the other person, affection, attention and such. But what is stimulated in you is your own feelings of love, your own being so full of brilliance, beauty, hope, and joy that you see beyond time and beyond worlds.

Sometimes the best you can do is put all of your pictures and beliefs into the experience of love, coloring and making it, to the best of your ability, fit your previous projections, forgetting that what you are experiencing is yourself. Whatever you do, a door has been opened. You may not be aware of what is going on, but you are aware that within you something great is happening. The great yet simple thing that is going on within you is the point at which you meet Great Spirit. In almost every instance, this is either forgotten or unknown.

When you experience love and meet Great Spirit, forgetting you are meeting Great Spirit, what happens within you creates all manner of projections and karmic entanglements from which you hopefully can learn. However, what if you ceased for a moment projecting that the love had something do with anyone or anything else and was simply a doorway inside of you to something unspeakably beautiful? What if you made a decision to find out more about that directly? What if?

If you decided to stop projecting your feelings of love onto someone else, you would find so much more than you ever could have possibly bargained to find. You would find at a certain point that it was impossible to distinguish whether the love was seemingly inside of you or outside of you. You would find yourself in quite a different universal construct, a realm where the metaphysical and physical become intertwined. Your sense of reality and your connection to it would have begun powerfully and dynamically to change.

The dynamic change in your reality would be toward opening to a powerful expression of divinity that exists within you in forms of light and color, beauty and spirit. You would find music, art, geometry, and other mathematics and seek to find a connection between these things and your life in the world. There would be a work in front of you to identify the link, your part in what you have identified, what actions you are to take, and what your role is within all the contexts that you have seen.

If you are sincere, and you will have to be very sincere to go that far, vital beings will begin to appear as instruments to show you the way. These beings will come in the form of persons, friends, enemies, lovers, teacher, and spirit beings. This is inevitable. You will start to think about how to live here in the truth of who you are and how to go to the source of this opening dynamic that is occurring within you. However, you do not get to that source through clamor, ambition, and fluffy positive thinking. What gets you to that source is your patient waiting. If you are not patient, you will become patient. You will be properly transmuted.

Those who have been transmuted through their sincerity and seeking, without their knowledge, will have begun the process of ascension. Their patience will take the form of a practice and of devotion, of being responsive and responsible toward the calling from within. Their mind will have begun to be converted. Their spirit, their heart shall have been made a lover of the Supreme.

Changes in the mind and the heart of the seeker will begin to appear in the external world. Without their knowing, the seeker will have slowly come to a point where the inner and the outer begin to become indistinguishable from each other. As a result, they consciously or unconsciously will seek the Divine and its expression in their external world, no matter what label it is given. Even those who think they are hopeless in terms of ever understanding anything will, at some point, know who they are and find a powerful experience. They will also begin to find that they are responsive and responsible to the inner call when Lords of Light appear to guide them home.

Azlo

Regarding this issue of men and women, the male energy and female energy, that is human. That is to say, human beings see things in terms of a masculine energy and a feminine energy, an evolution unique to this world. You believe women have a more cooperative spirit than men do and that men have a more demonstrative spirit than women do. That is a belief that has come out of the way people here on this earth evolved, but it is not a chemical disorder having to do with testosterone or with an energetic principle.

This being said, any distaste you may have for what men have done in this world should not be directed at men. It should be directed at the evil in men or else you will have no one to love. I must say however, women have not been involved in as much evil as men. However, there has been incredible confusion that exists in women as well as in men. In order to seek a defensive position, women, by and large, have emulated the darkness in men in a very basic kind of way and use awful seductions to achieve it. Men use seductions of a different type to lure women into their insanity. All of that must stop.

Seduction for security and sex has been completely perverted. It is an abomination. The seduction of men and women has a much higher purpose than control of women over men or men over women. Many things have been distorted, corrupted and perverted, and it is complete insanity.

Sun Bear

There are those who want relationships and are not in them and those who are in relationship, but not in the way they want to be in relationship. You may try for years and still have no relationship in the way you want. Well, maybe the relationship you want is something that you have already left behind in terms of where you are in the karmic continuum. In other words, maybe you want what you, think is a normal relationship, but find yourself frustrated by serial relationships that do not become permanent relationships or marriage relationships. Then this leaves you thinking there is something wrong with you.

There are many reasons why you may find yourself in one relationship after another that does not become permanent. However, I proffer to you that you may in fact be in a place in the karmic continuum where it is right to complete past relationships in the best way you are able. That is, souls with whom you have existing karmic ties in this plane of existence are the ones with whom you are completing through your serial relationships. These kinds of karmic completion relationships cannot be forced to go where you want them to go.

You are truly here in this world to complete your business. Therefore, with regard to relationships, you have to make certain determinations. Maybe you are in a relationship and there are children, but you want to end the relationship. You have decided that the relationship is not really meeting your needs for your life, but there is such a conflict in coming to close that relationship. Therefore, you feel it is important to complete the promise of your marriage or relationship. Maybe this leaves you feeling somewhat less satisfied than you imagine you would be if it were a different relationship, but you feel obligated to complete, either until the children are grown or until death do you part.

Maybe you are in love with a soul sibling, a soul brother or soul sister and it isn't as gratifying or as completing sexually as you want it to be, but you know this is the right relationship for you in terms of why you are here. You choose to see that relationship through because you feel it is right for your part of finishing relationship in this world. In addition, you see that to start another relationship would start another spiral into another karmic direction that opens a door instead of completing.

Perhaps you are at the stage of the journey where there are no more relationships to be had of the kind many other people have. Maybe for you, it is about moving on and completing all of your business here and that is why you are here in this world. This is something that is a revelation in the heart of the true seeker.

Another example may be that you are a monastic person who does not care for or want a relationship in this lifetime. You may be an Enunciate, one who gives things up, takes vows of chastity and poverty and that is your journey. This journey is not for everyone, but some are on this kind of a journey.

Whatever your path, it is not you who consciously decides where you are on the path and proclaims it as so, creating your own destiny, achieving your conscious goals. It just is not like that if you are truly ready to surrender to the Divine. You must find the truth of where you are with no more lies, if you are ready to see it, and with no more delusions.

First, you clear the decks so there is as little garbage as possible. Then you practice your meditations and service and live your life. You work, play, and enjoy your life, and you have contact with Spirit, allowing the Supreme Director to reveal to you the greater truth of who you are. Then you will find the greater truth of who you are is not a matter of restriction, but a matter of freedom. This is the path of joyous surrender. Great Spirit shows you how to surrender through your devotion, service, awakening, and seeking of the real truth, which can only be done with the humble 'I'.

Azlo

When love is a great principle amidst all people, love loses its need to posses. All that remains is a sense of permanent connection, which then is expressed in many ways.

Sun Bear

It is hard to accept that you can love without having agreement. However, you do not have to be in agreement to love unconditionally or to be loved unconditionally. The demand for love to be a particular way makes people crazy. That is not unconditional love, but is conditional love. Yes, any form of love is better than no love at all, even if the love is conditional.

However, if the aim is a soulful and unconditional love, that is what Great Spirit wants to reveal to those who are willing. Unconditional love is a love so great, so broad, so big, and so perfect that it has no conditions of agreement, disagreement or anything else. That kind of love is not generated at the level of humanity, but is generated above humanity, coming into human beings who submit themselves to receive it. This kind of love is what every human being wants.

As that kind of unconditional love comes to you, you will want to transmit it in proportion to the way you have received it.

Eventually you will want to transmit it in an unlimited way, and that is when you will face the challenge of the great masters. The challenge is a balance between forcing the unconditional love you have received upon others for their own sake, either individually or collectively, and allowing the love to teach you the way it teaches you, which is usually the acceptance of what is. It is very difficult for a human being to be in acceptance unless a greater power comes into you, a power like unto the Great Spirit.

Sun Bear

It is not possible to live without causing hurt or being hurt. That is why the path is about acceptance and forgiveness, not about perfection. If the path were about perfection, nobody could do it. Not only that, but if you did live in an existence that was absolutely without flaw, by whose judgment is it flawless? By what standard does one derive the definition of flawless? Therefore, in part, you are human to learn how to love unconditionally and to forgive and to accept.

Azlo

Sensuality is always an opening to something beyond your current mind. In your world, you are just beginning to emerge in this way, and this is why you are advancing so far scientifically of late.

Merlin

Wherever there is love, there is that which holds elements of what you are all about and what you seek. When I speak of love, I mean something more like power, the life force, that which is life itself and the source of all other things. This force can trigger emotions in you that you like and some you may label love. However, I am not speaking about all of those emotions that are triggered and flow through your being that bliss you out, warm you, heal you, and inspire you. I am talking about that which is the source of all of those feelings and emotions.

What all seek is like love. Wherever there is that which is like love, there you will find a guiding light, a teaching light, and a great opportunity. The opportunity is to learn that which shall help you either in that moment or later become discriminating about what is the source and what it is you seek.

Sun Bear

It is very possible and quite easy to forget that you come here to learn, especially when you are in the middle of a relationship and things are not going well. The attitude might become, is this relationship the right relationship for me? How can I get what I want? Why am I like this in relationship? Why is my partner like that? These questions are about fixing or changing the relationship, yourself or your partner when it is about something much simpler than that. It is about learning love, which often has to do with acceptance and letting go more than it has to do with anything else.

Merlin

Most people think everyone deserves love. Not everyone gets it, but of course, everyone deserves love, and everyone wants it in one form or another. However, let us presume your journey is to include relationship and you are a conscious, spiritual soul, a seeker, and a finder. Let us say you find a relationship that seems to hold great opportunity and promise. It fits everything you understand yourself to be about as a conscious, loving, God embracing, soulful being. This is it for you, so to speak. You know that things do not necessarily always go the way you want them to go, but you also know that you have some sort of influence over which way things go. You are of course masterful sufficient to be able to remain as conscious as possible, and will do your best to value such an enterprise as this, it being such a great opportunity.

However, let us say you are not aware of some things that are so astoundingly simple that you think you have transcended the possibility of being caught or motivated at those levels. Take for example security, prestige, sex, power, control, influence or acceptance. Whatever it may be, these normal human animal motives have a purpose. They have a bright side and a dark side to them, and you have learned all of those things as a conscious entity. You are going to be much more aware of those things. In fact, since you have had all of those lessons already, you know what you are doing, and this is really about love.

Do you presume you have understood these basic things or do you remain alert to the fact that you are still a human being in a human body? Do you presume that at any time natural motives to the human animal my simply spontaneously evidence themselves at will, not because you want them to, not because you have failed or succeeded in mastering the 'ins' and 'outs' of such instincts, but simply because you remain a fleshy being, vulnerable to the fleshy attitudes?

Let us say that some aspect of your animal nature is so poignant that you cannot overcome it sufficiently to appreciate what is available in a certain experience such as a loving relationship. You want to overcome it, but you simply cannot. In this instance, it is terribly convenient to tell yourself that you are beyond it. That would give you further permission to indulge yourself freely and at will without the need to be conscious of anything except to somehow manipulate, unwittingly or without mastery, your end.

What do I mean by manipulate your end? Let us take the idea of prestige because it is a part of the social instinct of the human animal. That is, all human beings have a need to be social. Some human beings resent that need because it forces them to engage in interactions with other human beings, just for the purpose of their own survival, when they really would rather not encounter a human being if they do not have to encounter them. However, human beings do have an instinct for some sort of social interaction because they know their survival depends upon it. If you are going to have social interactions, why not have the most prestigious social interactions that potentially avail you to the greatest reward? Perhaps, if you are in a prestigious enough position, there will be more resource, money, recognition, and sense of self-worth and all of those things that go along with prestige.

Perhaps you think, "I am not after prestige so that I can secure my life, utilizing some man or woman simply to make myself feel better about myself. I am aware of those things, and I am beyond that. I look for something bigger than that." On the other hand you may think, "These things are normal, natural things that I would be very stupid not to consider as a part of what I include in my prospects for relationship. I must give it its necessary value." You could be at any point in-between these two examples. At this point, we are presuming this discussion is going on inside of all masterfully developing conscious beings who have some sense of self and self-worth, some sense of direction and true awareness of identity. At least let us presume this for the sake of argument.

Being of the mind that you may be aware of or not vulnerable to some sort of untoward consequence from your instinctual drive, you go about trying to address the instinctual drive in the manner you think most appropriate. But let us say that there is a lack of true understanding of the instinctual drive or that it is so disguised as to be unrecognizable to you. Let us say that maybe your daddy did not pay enough attention to you and you never felt enough acknowledgements. Maybe mommy did not hold you enough and you never felt sufficient connection. Maybe your big sister was jealous and tried to hurt or kill you. Maybe your big brother beat you up all of the time. Maybe your family did not have sufficient resource to take care of you in the way you thought and felt you truly deserved. Maybe the demands upon you were too strong or too little.

Whatever it might be for you, somehow the particular instinct of prestige, which you think you have handled or have in right perspective, is not as rightly handled as you think. In fact, in this particular example, for the sake or argument, prestige may be the primary drive responsible for your thinking you are in love with a person. That is, the person you think you are in love with represents the single most important missing aspect in your life.

The love, nurture, and affection you need flows so easily from this person or in the presence of this person, that prestige is not even an issue because it is being so readily addressed.

However, what if that redress goes away? Of course, at first you may not worry about such a thing. Then a month, a year, two years, ten years or twenty years into your intimate relationship you have been on the receiving end of a few things from your partner that lead you to believe your great need in this area is not as satisfied as you might have initially thought. What do you do then, run away or try to get what you want?

The popular spiritualized respond of today would be, "I do not look for my needs to be addressed from another person. I look for them from within myself or rise above such things. I realize that I am an eternal spirit in truth, and only bear the illusion of the physical body. I understand the needs of the physical body often portray some unnecessary delusion that I cannot even become caught up in, so I shall rise above it." Of course, usually it is the man in the relationship who tries to rise above it saying such things as "I am above this. You should be above this." Things like "I could never satisfy her needs. I have given everything to this woman. She is an empty, bottomless pit, and no matter what I do it is never enough," or some such version of this. The woman's version is "Maybe if I give just a little more this way, then he will give just a little more that way. Maybe if I am just a little more of this, he will be just a little more of that."

Meanwhile all of this dynamic has filtered into what was initially your conscious journey into an exploration you were fully aware had pitfalls. However, you were just exploring this area because you thought there was a meaningful chance to experience the love you deserve, the spiritual expression as manifest through another being or through you, or that is what you told yourself. Alternatively, you were looking for the opportunity to be able to proclaim, "Look what I have created with my spiritual development. I have manifested the perfect response to my spiritual needs in this partner." That is how the natural animal instinct of prestige comes into play in relationship.

Yeshua, Enoch, St. Germaine

All relationships, including loving relationships, change form. They come to an end, whether that end is at the end of life or at the three, five, six or one hundred year point. Human beings hope, depend on, and have faith in an arbitrary definitive that says until the end of life we shall remain together. So long as we endure this world, we promise to commit to the love of each other.

However, in truth, souls have no such regard, having no interest in the world and relationships. When a soul meets another at the level of soul, there is intrigue at the beginning and satisfaction and completion. Satisfaction and completion occurs because soul, in its purest stage, is contented to know its companion. When a soul is with another soul who wants contentment and is not yet content, meaning in the presence of a soul they love and yet they feel incomplete, dissatisfied, wanting, and needing, it has not reached the level of soul fulfillment that is available to the soul, either as an individual or as a couple.

A soul is more easily able to connect with those souls referred to as soul mates. However, if a soul projects too much worldly need upon a soul mate, a soul mate will not long last. The assumptions, both positive and negative, born of need projection from a human being's pain will not encumbered a soul mate. The soul mate will feel only too happy to give. Whereas another soul, who is not a soul mate, will be burdened by the needs of another human being who is not their soul mate.

Yet there are also those who think and fool themselves that they are giving while in fact what they are doing is seducing. They are giving because they wish something in return. The giving is not giving at all, but a device of seduction to appropriate or manipulate what one desires from another. This is not love, but subterfuge. It is the source of a great many sicknesses that are learned from generation to generation, for which one should not be judged. One should however be aware of and remember the worldly reason why human beings, men and women, come together, which is to survive and endure the world. This thinking or dynamic is strong in the human culture. How often does one say something like, this person would be right if only they were smart enough, rich enough, powerful enough or beautiful enough? Enough for what? Enough for what you need in order to address what it takes for you to live with an intact ego structure?

The soul does not work on that level at all. In fact, it works at almost the opposite level. The soul comes with a love for comfort and a love for truth. It immediately demonstrates this regardless of whatsoever one decides shall be the nature of a relationship in terms of worldly convention. That is, in terms of until the end of life or not until the end of life, whether man and woman, woman and woman, man and man, it does not matter. The soul does not even care at what level one engages in terms of family. A soul mate may be your brother, your mother, your father or your cousin. A soul mate may be a criminal, a highly empowered soul, a great soul or a master teacher. Soul does not regard worldly convention.

If you are on the path of truth, you must understand something very important. You must seek to keep your connections with those whom you love simple, for they can quickly grow complex if you do not. You must stay out of the need to define the relationship by one context or another or soon your mastery will destroy your definition. You must aim to be at peace within yourself and be in acceptance and appreciation, not only with your love, but also with how another who loves you may feel. More than anything else, you must engender and cultivate trust. Trust that is already there is good, but it is not enough. You must further engender trust, and further cultivate it. What you give is your loving trust.

How you give your loving trust is based upon your wisdom. Some must do things that are decidedly not soulful to engender trust, even though it may not be the highest things. Some make promises and contracts of all kinds. A soul cannot be contracted or promised, but in order to engender trust, often this is done. However, this must not be mistaken for love. This is simply what souls may do to foster the growth of love, for remember the movement of love is from lesser, more needful understanding of one another to greater understanding of one another.

It may seem at the beginning that love initially swells, but love is simply narrower at the beginning, even though one is perhaps at great joy of the prospect of what may lie ahead. And as that which lies ahead becomes more present in the now, love has a demand that you grow in your ability to understand, to love, and trust. That love will be asked to grow more expansive, for love asks of you more than what you intend for it to ask of you and what it initially appears to ask of you.

There will be those who demand of you and you will demand of others. This cannot foster love. In fact, it will disable love. When love becomes a demand, even a righteous demand, love cannot grow there. Love can only be freely given. Therefore that which you do to foster and grow love, whether familial or romantic, has to do with how capable you feel at engendering and giving your trust and love.

If you do not feel capable of extending love and trust, it is wise to cultivate that first, to the extent that you can, before you enter into attempting to do that. This is [particularly so with family, for families often have grown intolerant and unforgiving, having become quite familiar with each other at certain points in time. Therefore, if family is unforgiving and you seek to engender connection with them, if your intent is love rather than to reprimand or hurt, then you had best come with the ability to forgive or develop that ability to the extent that you can.

The purpose of love outside of family is to enable you toward more intimate love, even within family, and then beyond it. Whatever conditions in your family may have fostered hurt, pain, suffering, and degradation of your own soul nature must first be addressed and amended through relationships outside of family. This is contrary to popular thinking, but must be done before one can carry love back to the family.

This then is what we say. You must bring trust and you must receive from another their willingness to trust in you. You must bring trust and you must receive trust if you wish to be with a soul mate that goes until the end of your life and further. Love has its own course, not defined by the beginnings and endings of death, for death is not what it appears to be. In terms of your family, if you cannot bring that that engenders trust, then work further. If you cannot bring forgiveness, then work further.

Pray for those who are particularly difficult or who challenge you the most greatly, then you may see a change if you pray that they receive their own growth and healing. It is necessary to love your enemy, that is to give them the love of your thinking, your heartfelt well-being, that they may prosper by the will of God, by the will of all that is good around them. In that healing of their sickness their difficulty toward you shall dissipate and your relationship shall grow miraculously well. This is what to do if you cannot bring trust and forgiveness. Pray that they grow more in their wholeness. Pray as though they were a sick person in need of what makes them well, if that is what they wish, for in fact it may only be their sickness that has hurt you, even as your sickness may have hurt them.

This is an important step to be able to go forward in love with those with whom there has been difficulty in relationship. However, when there are persons who are intimates in relationship, such as lovers and family, it requires more than simply going on in love if one desires a greater closeness and a greater growth. Love is important, but it requires that one hear what is being said by those who have difficulty with you. It requires acknowledging the truth of the difficulty and making changes where one may indeed be resistant or even not believe that such things could be true.

Sometimes it is difficult to hear an awful truth about oneself. Sometimes when this comes, and it does come in the life of all people, all that it does is serve to cause that person to enter into a pattern of self-hatred, rejection, and defensiveness. However, what if there are truly some ugly things about you? How beautiful is the soul who can recognize its own ugliness and change, for the ugliness is but a pattern, a sickness that needs to be addressed. It often is not caused by any fault of one's own. Nevertheless, one is left with the responsibility of addressing it within their self, even though one may not have created the problem.

There are things that people may do to survive that are decidedly ugly. Even though you may have left behind certain ugliness, after recognizing it and making changes, sometimes there are still consequences of the past you must face. This is inevitable. Often this occurs between intimates over long periods, whether they are family or lovers. You cannot forget the past and heal it without seeking to address it at times, and it cannot be addressed unless it is acknowledged. If it is not acknowledged, there can be no forgiveness on the part of most human beings unless there is also an amends, even if amends may be impossible.

To seek to put things right where there is a wrong is to be accountable as a soul. If a soul wishes to truly understand and embrace a transition into a higher consciousness, a soul must stand accountable, because this is the only way one can forgive the self. What is there to forgive if you are not accountable? If there is nothing to forgive, then you are perfect. If you are perfect, what is the need for forgiveness? If there is no need for forgiveness, how can you love unconditionally?

Unconditional love implies that sooner or later you will have to love yourself and others irrespective of conditions and circumstances. However, you cannot demand this from another. One cannot impose this upon another against their will. Unconditional love stems from accountability. Only in the presence of accountability, can there be forgiveness and love that is unconditional. Think hard upon this.

Sun Bear

People usually get married because it looks like their needs will be mutually met by each other. However, inevitably people grow and change. Before you know it somebody is not giving the other one what they want or need. That is usually when one or the other partner moves on. They let go of the demand that the other person be what they expect. What is incredible is to find love at this point of letting go and beyond the letting go.

One who moves on from a relationship because their needs are not being met will very likely find someone else who does address their needs. However, in truth people can only address each other's needs to a certain point. Once those needs are addressed to the point they can be addressed, that need fulfillment will appear to not be enough.

One will eventually come to understand that they are here for something more than needs fulfillment. They will start to see that there is something else to be done for the achievement of fulfillment and completion. Therefore, when it comes to commitments in marriage or lifelong relationships, it is only going to be lifelong and successful if both persons can choose to expand the ways they love to the point of acceptance.

Merlin

Anyone is able to give service at any moment, no matter what aspects of your character may or may not have been refined. You are able to do this because something devotional and beautiful occurs between you and the Divine. The Divine gives you a gift, which is actually a gift of love, and makes you a lover of the Divine. A dance goes on between you and the Divine, the Divine separating itself from you enough to have a relationship with you, and then the Divine goes back and becomes you. It is a little dance going back and forth between oneness and separation because relationships are beautiful and because you have given loving service.

Sun Bear

In your society, relationships that culminate in marriage and children have traditionally not been based on love. They have been based instead upon survival and the continuance of progeny and family structure. The instinct, aware or unaware, is to continue the species and to extend yourself or elements of yourself into life after you are no longer here. This is a very strong instinct.

Naturally, tribes and even nations have an investment in the healthy development of such progeny because the tribe or nation depends upon it. This has so much been the tradition that it is only in the past hundred or so years that people have began to think about marrying for love, if they marry at all. When marriage is for survival, then it is about who is the best hunter, has the most money, can make the best children, and is the most attractive and intelligent. One instinctually chooses a partner based upon what they imagine will provide the best possibility for survival. That is, a choice of partners becomes a need-based function that allows continuance, which is not love. This is why people were promised in marriage and exchanged dowries for women. It was an attempt to focus on the survival of a people. The luxury of love was insufficient and less important than survival.

You may think that today it is all about love and not survival. However, how many people become divorced because there is not enough money, no sexual relations or one person is not strong enough or there cannot be children? These are needs projected on another about survival. In addition, certainly you would have difficulty choosing a lifetime partner who has an IQ so low you would consider them retarded. You might think you could not communicate with them. You would be concerned with your future, your position in society, appearances, how you might be held back, and all kinds of matters of security.

Trying to have a relationship based upon love is one matter. However, when you want a relationship to become permanent, then you begin to think about your future and your survival. The more spiritual you become, the more you find out that you have to base a relationship on letting go of certain things if you are to remain together. You have to base a relationship on acceptance of each other, as you are if you want to continue to love.

Many people stay together because they would rather survive than have love. Some people grow to love, but coming to love and remaining in love is essentially a new idea. Until recently in the global culture, there has not been the luxury to consider anything other than survival. That instinct for survival has been passed on to you, in your genes and in the way you were raised. You were taught to look for and expect certain things in a partnership. Some of these things you saw on television, read in books, and have parental influence toward, and that colors your perceptions in terms of what you look for in romantic love relationships.

In the Native American culture, there is a hand clasping ceremony, which is like a marriage. There is also a letting go ceremony much like a divorce. These things were done in ways as to help people let go. In your culture divorce is a very rude and terrible thing that destroys families and makes it hard for children to recover. Lately mediation has been introduced, which is a step better than divorce. Divorce is simply the attack of the lawyers, two dogs fighting each other until everybody is ripped apart.

Why is it difficult for two people graciously to let go? It is because image is involved and society, money, and emotional, and physical security. Human instincts are programmed to protect and defend for survival. When survival appears to be threatened, you will fight to the death for your survival as much as you need to, and then have many negative feelings and wounds.

When an individual or a culture begins to progress emotionally and spiritually, people begin to see things differently. This is what is now beginning to happen in your culture. One thing that is changing is that women do not like to be seen as chattel. In your culture, women have only had the right to vote in the 20th century. Women could not get an education until recently. In addition, only men could own property. All of these things kept men more powerful than women, with women having to submit to a degree or fight in order to get their needs met.

Traditionally the agreement has been that women give sex and children and men give protection and material. This is all about instinct, and when relations do not lead in the direction of the instinctual demand, then that is where the problems begin. That is where people begin to take offense and manipulation and dishonesty starts to figure into the equation. That is where selfishness and inconsiderateness come into play and fear takes root.

The moment there is sex involved or the moment you begin to relate to another person according to their projected gender associations, then all kinds of things begin to figure in, and it can become a very, very confusing matter. By gender associations, I do not necessarily mean sexual relationships between men and women, women and women, and men and men. I also mean relationships between a father and a son, a mother and a father, a daughter and a father, a daughter and a mother and between siblings. The moment you begin to project conscious or unconscious gender associations upon each other the whole matter of sex relations becomes a battle for the survival of the fittest, except to the extent that you can understand the consciousness we call love and let it come into play more greatly than the instinct for survival.

There are many, many blind spots, especially where instinct is already in control. For example, you have a built-in mechanism to breathe. If you do not breathe, your instinct to breathe does it for you anyway. What if that automatic mechanism stopped working and you had then to be conscious of every single breath in order to trigger the mechanism for breathing? In the same way, how are you going to be conscious of a place where your instinct for survival is an automatic mechanism? Your attention is not on the automatic mechanism, but on many other things.

Sex and gender associations are an automatic mechanism. Emotions are what mask your perception of this patterned mechanism. You justify the beliefs that you have around gender associations with emotions, while below that there is simply survival instinct. Therefore, the places to uncover your instinctual survival mechanisms regarding gender orientation and sex are the places most obvious for you to see. Then you can allow the consciousness of these places to seep in deeper and deeper. Become aware first of the most obvious and glaring aspects of your persona as relates to sex, and as you hold these places in consciousness other aspects of your own survival mechanism will start to reveal themselves to you.

You may start to notice shame, which is like profound guilt, when you first start to explore you blind spots. Shame is like self-punishment that comes after you feel guilty. Guilt is first, and then shame comes later because you know you are guilty and you sentence yourself. The self-sentence is shame, like a self-hatred that goes very deep. When shame comes relative to your body, it can come in any number of superficial ways that can be very debilitating. The way shame comes most deeply is when you disregard the cultural standards because your body, sex, and emotions are all tied up in the cultural standards.

As an example, there is something we call the Adam and Eve syndrome. The woman uses the promise of sex and the man uses the promise of security to get their needs met by each other. The man learns to manipulate with protection and comfort. The woman learns to manipulate using sexual gratification of the man. This is not who people are, but there is an instinct used to get what you want. Not only is it instinct, but it is passed along in the culture.

There is tremendous pressure from the culture that, even when a soul does not wish to participate, there is still a pull to think and behave in the socially prescribed manners. The result is that all kinds of misunderstandings begin to happen because you have very little power to exert the higher truth. A man might say, "I can give love and I do not care so much about how a woman looks or how sexy she is, just whether she has this great thing inside." Then he is in partnership and there is no sex or she puts on fifty pounds or he wants children and she cannot have any, and he says, "Now wait a minute." She, on the other hand, may want someone to give her things, and the man does not make enough money. This makes the man feel either angry or inadequate, and he may not want to feel inadequate or angry.

In reaction to the various things going on in the relationship the man may start looking for a woman whom he thinks does not care about money. That is a reaction to a pattern and not a pure consciousness. He may start looking for a woman whom he thinks has a good libido. It is a patterned reaction for his survival instinct, and he is looking for security.

I have told this story many times, but I remember specifically that when it came to women the last time I was here, I just did not trust very easily. However, one day I was so lonely that I prayed to Great Spirit. "Great Spirit, I am a man. You know what I need," and in a very short time, about a week, a woman came to my door and said, "Sun Bear, I have to be with you." I thanked Great Spirit over and over for sending this woman.

It was not too long before I was saying to Great Spirit, "Take her away." This was not because anything was wrong with her. There was just something that began to occur with which I could not cope. It was all of those things that happen between men and women in relationship, which was what I was used to experiencing. In other words, my patterns started happening all over again, and I started to remember why I had no woman in the first place. Great Spirit heard my prayers to take her away, because a few days later the woman said to me, "Sun Bear, I have to go." I cried and cried. I did not want her to go, but it was right for her to go or else she would not have said that.

What was that all about? I want a woman. Take her away. I want her again. Do you know how much confusion can grow in a person around experiences like that? How can you focus on a spiritual journey when instinctual demands from your human animal nature, including your sexual nature, are complicating your mind and emotions unbeknownst to you? So first you have got to open your eyes and see what is running the show for you. See where your blind spots might be.

Merlin

If you want love in your life, in whatever form, you cannot save your love up for one person. You need to start making loving bonds with more and more people. This will draw to you the one that you need to have in your life, just by making loving bonds with others.

It is always better to attract a lover than to look for a lover. It is always better to be the loved one rather than always to be the one looking for a lover or trying to hold on to a loved one. The way to do that is to express love. The way to create love is to make more love. Help people to make their lives more loving, and it gets better and better for you.

It is always a good sign when there are people around you to love and to whom you can turn. You do not have to accept every amorous advance, but it is always good when you see love extended toward you from different directions.

Another thing about love is that all entities willing to embrace unconditional and unreasonable love shall know an eternal state of being that is without pain. By unreasonable love, I mean loving even when there is no reason to love and loving even when there is reason. Those who are willing to embrace unreasonable and unconditional love more and more shall utterly heal themselves. Their nature shall grow more and more into eternal beings.

There is no reason whatsoever that people have to love. In certain circumstances, there are many good reasons for people not to love. However, it is only when love becomes unreasonable that people start to see elements of truth.

As far as the pain and the suffering that people go through, there is an answer to this, at least for human beings. Because the Great Spirit never expected there to be pain, and yet there are numbers of entities who struggle, suffer, and experience pain, something was created to address that suffering. That something is that God comes in the form of a personality who has great power, in a sense, to rescue the desperate.

Sometimes God comes to a person as a form of energy or as God itself. Nevertheless, it is something that person's mind can embrace as a personal form of God, through which they then become devoted. Only those who have devotion can be rescued. The Lord of the Universe is the power that is working in the universe that comes to address the need of the desperate. It can manifest itself in any number of forms that are very personal to the one who reaches for it.

Sun Bear

Love is not something you get. It is something you give. This is very hard for human beings because they want to get love, but love is about what you give. In order to give love you must touch an inner resource that is like an endless well, and then you can give and give. You do not give in such a way as is a sacrifice where you give and have nothing left until you are completely drained. No. The love of which I speak is given freely and creates abundance all around you and within you, though first, you must touch an unlimited inner resource in order to give in that way.

One way to give love is by contribution to society. Contribute what makes life beautiful, exciting, easy, rewarding, and comfortable. Contribute that which promotes growth and intelligence. Giving to the culture in such ways as accentuates and develops these things causes the culture to reward you. If the culture is made happy by individuals giving for the mutual benefit of all, then the giver is rewarded by the culture giving to them, and everyone benefits. This is one way to express love.

Imhotep

Of all that is important the most important thing is the primary focus upon the power of love. It does not matter what you think love is or is not. What matters is that you cultivate thoughts and inclinations toward love.

At some point, the power that love is will make you uncomfortable because love is a power that must be embraced in your entire being, and brings the force of life. To that extent you allow love to be present in your being and in your body you can know radiant existence, health, and aliveness. To that extent that you do not know the power of love, you experience a diminishment of life forces. Therefore, by merely focusing upon the principle of what love is you embrace the very power of life, of love. This power is something that is always with you and makes your mind clear and your destiny open to you.

The power that love is must be the focus that guides all forms of spirituality. Many wish to know which disciplines will open the doors of the various planes and chakras to mystical experiences. It is not the technique or discipline that opens these doors, but the focus upon the love in your heart. No matter what your practices, techniques or which doors you wish to open, where you first focus upon your heart center you will begin to feel a relaxing of the physical body and a gentleness of spirit. In a short time, that gentleness of spirit will expand into a great feeling of love, warmth, and safety. Any discipline practiced within the presence of that power is practiced within the presence of love. In the presence of this love doors that would not open before will then open to you.

Sun Bear

In your cultures, most biological parents raise their own children. However, what if they did not raise their own children and instead left it to others whose expertise was raising children? This would create a different psychology between a mother and father, father and daughter, mother and daughter, father and son, and mother and son, an entirely different psychology of family structure.

First, it would cause those who are outside of the bloodline to be considered as valuable as those within the bloodline are. Those within the bloodline would also be considered valuable because they are genetically connected to the bloodline. In addition, this would create different partnership relationships because the first love of a child would not necessarily be the mother and father, but instead would be the caretaker. When the child was old enough and smart enough, then the child would recognize the value of their parents for genetically contributing to them, becoming grateful for this contribution.

The result would be an entirely different psychology and different ways of looking at romantically oriented relationships. There would be less need for the individual to look at another individual as his or her property or possession. Hence, partners would not be bound to each other as in current style marriages. Bonding and connection would occur, but not binding in the same way as human beings currently tend to have an affinity toward their own bloodlines, races, and national and cultural groupings. Instead, children would be raised on the basis of an expertise, and their society would evolve on a basis of what is a logical empirical structure of the society, including many forms of support and opportunity for individuals.

This is a much more open way of looking at the culture. All begin to learn that the society is set up in such a way as everybody contributes to the one and the one contributes to everybody. There is a great passion derived from being part of that kind of culture, particularly because life can be so filled with beauty and happiness that individuals want to live forever. They have a desire to contribute to society and they are richly rewarded for their contribution.

Francesco (St. Francis of Assisi)

Love is not sacrifice. There is no room in this world anymore for the benefit of one at the expense of another, for this does not advance the human condition. Rather there is room for gifts, self-awakening, mutual support, self-empowerment, and cooperation amongst each other that benefit all without one costing that another might benefit. These kinds of arrangements must start with you dedicating time and energy toward yourself. This will have attendant to it many kinds of feelings that you sometimes are alone and cut off from the world.

Perhaps relationships of the romantic kind are your greatest desire. These relationships may sometimes seem to elude you or elude the level of satisfaction you wished. That is because the satisfaction you wish does not come from a relationship, but from the self that you have denied for all of this time. Even if there had been a romantic relationship, you would not experience the fulfillment that could be there until you have dedicated the time to being selfish as well as selfless. In these times, which can be lonely, are the aspects of the path that one must walk alone, no matter what else is said or thought.

Therefore, the time for sacrifice is over. The time for giving from a place of richness within your being is now here. This can only come from having first given to the self.

Sun Bear, Great Bear, Sam Strong Body & Chief Great White Eagle

Sexuality is connected to the life force. Sex is what brings bodies into the world. There is power in the vagina, penis, semen, egg, and everything that has to do with sex and sexuality. It represents your lust for living, juiciness, passion for whatever you do every single day. It has everything to do with your enthusiasm, creativity, and beauty. In a way, it is how you manifest the divine physically. There are a lot of ways to express the divine. However, when you have the power to make a life in your body, whether you choose to do it or not, it is a tremendous power that nearly everybody has.

In our teachings, if you want to be healthy, you have to have sex. In our religion if a person does not have sex, they are either unhealthy or they have a very different calling with another purpose, which is very rare. Therefore, if someone never has sex, most of the time there is something very wrong, and it needs to be investigated and addressed.

In your culture, if you have been surrounded by healthy appreciation of natural beauty and sexuality, you are very fortunate, because it is not very popular in your culture. Understand that the dominant culture first introduced in this nation were the Puritans. Many came to visit our Nation, but your culture is primarily an extension of the Puritans, who had some very mixed up ideas about sex. That is not the only culture that came here, but when it comes to sexual attitudes, for some reason the puritanical position on sex seems to be what has been the outgrowth of your sexual society. Puritanism took hold more than other cultures, some of which were sexually much healthier than the puritanical point of view. Thus, it is rare to be surrounded by people with healthy sexual attitudes.

The mind is very popular in your culture. The body is thought of in a very vain manner, as a point of vanity, not in a spiritual manner that is healthy and integrated. The fire of the spirit in your nation is very strong, and that is good. Your emotional body is very healthy, even though it is a little wild and untamed. These are elements of what is important for human beings in our religion. It is really five forces of energy that are important, life force energy found in sexuality, air as in the mind, fire as in the spirit, water as in the emotions, and energy in motion as in your physical body.

In our religion, Great Spirit expresses itself through something like a circle. Within the circle is a black void, a black hole, where creation begins with a spark of life emerging from the black hole. We see this black hole as the feminine space and the spark as the masculine. The black hole represents implosion and the spark of life represents an explosion, similar to inhalation and exhalation. Breath is an important part of our sexual teachings.

The life force that creates and continues the universe is expressed, in our belief, through the sexual nature. In alignment with the sexual nature, you are able to express the power of the universe. This is why the experience of the power of the energy in sex is so incredible, at least at some points in your life. If you are not feeling that, it is because culturally there are elements of the puritanical idea that have created a reaction in you causing repression, either directly in your own psyche or in the psyches of those who raised and taught you. You received some sort of twisted idea that you could not accept related to your body and sex. Rather than accept the twisted idea your body or psyche has shut down.

Shutting down of the psyche is what occurs in early societies like yours. Your society is only a few hundred years old compared to our society that is at least two thousand years old. The East Indian society is over five thousand years old. The Semitic people's society, which is very disjointed, goes back over seven thousand years. Chinese society goes back six or seven thousand years. Compared to this, your society has a long way to go, because many people in your society reflect the attitudes of a young society with its numerous psychic twists.

It is important to be both spiritual and sexual, which are a part of the same thing. Your sexual energy is the way to restore youthfulness and vigor to your being. There is no other way to restore youth and vigor without your sexual energy being a part of it, when it is properly used. Sexuality, in our religious understanding, is important for your physical health and your state of mind. Sexual sensitivity, awareness, arousal, and desires that take place within your body are what make your body a sacred temple. Without sexual expression most people will just wither up, disconnect, and become isolated. Therefore, it is important to have this as a regular part of your being.

If your sexual energy is closed off, it behooves you to educate and heal yourself in the area of sex. If you do not do this, you cannot be well in all areas of your life. This is how important it is. In our religion sex does not necessarily mean with the opposite sex partner or with any partner. You must be able to masturbate and enjoy your body. You must be able to have a deep pleasure in your body one way or another. If there is not pleasure, then you know that this is something that needs your attention.

The holders of the sexual wisdom in our culture were the fire women or fire men. Fire women were chosen by the wizened grandmothers and were the holders of the sexual secrets. Usually they were women whose sexual vitality was very strong because their duty and service would be to have sex every single day, which they loved to do. The medicine women and the grandmothers would get together and raise the fire women to be able instructors of sexuality to their nations. This was how it was done.

In your society, fire women are very identifiable. Most often, they are in positions such as sexual surrogates, sex therapists or even call girls. The fire women can be in the mystery schools, undercover, but they are identifiable because they thrive on the vitality of their physical bodies. They love their bodies. They love their fire. They love their energy. They love all of this about themselves, even if other people do not understand. Sometimes they become disheartened because people do not understand this.

The fire men are also easily identifiable. First, they love women. They love themselves, but they also love women. They do not abuse women. They just love women, and are usually very honest and open about their feelings. Even if they want to, they cannot bind themselves to one woman because they are not meant to be with one woman. Fire men will tell you outright that their purpose is to heal and free women. They are freed by sexuality or they feel they free someone else by sexuality.

Fire women and men genuinely and sincerely love their work and they think of it as a service. Their job is to restore life into society and usually they give this service to deadened men and women. Fire women and men are the holders and keepers of the sexual healing ways and they have been for centuries. These people know this because they feel it in their bones.

People who absolutely recognize this as their service feel there is accountability to the universe. They feel they must do some work every day on a sexual level to heal themselves and others. It is a commitment to a truth they know about themselves. If they deny the commitment or are not fully true to the commitment, they will find that almost always something seems to go awry in their lives. This is a very powerful calling for those who are the fire people, the holders of the knowledge of the sexual ways.

Sun Bear

The inability to have an orgasm has to do with control, control over your own psyche, your universe, your own being, and safety with cultivating intimacy, which is an extraordinary challenge in deep and profound love. That is to say, if you are in love with someone and become more and more intimate, eventually you will have difficulty reaching sexual orgasms. Even if you easily reach orgasms, the level of intimacy will sooner or later challenge your physiology.

In other words, if you have had some physiological or psychic connection that first triggers orgasmic states, intimacy will take you deeper. Sooner or later you will contact fear and the need for growth. Your body and psyche will shut down and will have eventually to open at a new level. In fact, the reason some people rarely or never have a sexual orgasm is because they have reached the limit of their ability to experience intimacy.

The purpose of love relationships is taking people beyond their limits of intimacy, if they choose. A person has to be willing to embrace love as a growth experience and not as a perfect opportunity for happiness. If a person forgets about the prefect opportunity for THE one to have happiness and instead embraces any relationship as an opportunity for growth, they will proceed much faster in having orgasms.

Sun Bear

Tribes are formed on the basis of need, not on the basis of love. Communism cannot work because it is formed on the basis of need. Its intention is to be compassionate, but it is all based around need, and need leads to despair and desperation. Love is that which flows forth from prosperity and abundance, a very different principle.

Groups must form, not based upon what they can get, but upon what they can give. This formation of groups comes from individuals being self-aware and self-empowered so that the individuals know who they are, therefore empowering themselves to give. It is a very simple principle, the principle of love.

In this country, those who fear communist ideals fear them because they know communism, like capitalism, turns into a greed-based or a fear-based society. To these same people the idea of love and cooperation sounds antiquated and perhaps even naïve. However, sooner or later individuals must come to know that they have to focus on giving and on cooperation, putting aside fear-based demands.

People often approach interactions with others, especially love relationships, from a place of their own need and whether or not those needs will be met. Love can never exist with that approach because that is more like a business arrangement, which is alright, but is not love. Love relationships are based upon beings not looking for what they can get, but whether or not there is an outlet for and receptivity to what they have to give and therefore a high probability of cooperation. That requires an individual know and believe in their gift or that which they are here to give that proliferates throughout their life. That is what they must give.

Merlin

You cannot have a relationship with God. People do not always understand that, but to have a relationship with God there has to be two of you, God and you. What happens when you have a union with God is that there is no relationship. You have oneness and the relationship disappears. What that means, the mind will be trying to figure out for centuries to come.

Sun Bear

In order to have a relationship, other than simply having a sort of casual friendship with a little sex in it, you need to be ready to enter into a situation of give and take and compromise. In order to do that, you must be very strong in who you are without losing yourself.

In this day and age, for a woman to be strong in who she is without losing herself, it is not something that is so easily found. This is because men tend to look for their mommies or look for someone for whom they can be a father. Rarely is it that a man is looking for an equal.

The way that you create or bring to you an equal in partnership is by working out the day-to-day aspects of your life to the point you feel you have a balance, meaning enough money, time, pleasure, and spirituality. When such a balance is created, a partner shall walk through the door that is an equal. It will not be someone who is a lopsided compliment to give you something that you do not feel you have within yourself or someone looking to you to fill what they do not have within themselves, which is an unequal relationship.

Merlin

To really love someone in an unconditional sense means loving that they are different than you, appreciating, recognizing, respecting, and enjoying the differences as well as what you have in common. That cannot take place when there are large wounded places inside of you that have a need to be met by the other in a particular manner. Unconditional love takes place only when you honor each other's differences and make a great deal of room to be very creative about how you choose to go about it, living in the moment and respecting each other's love. That is absolutely beautiful, and is a sacred union.

Philos

Most people do not have the courage to face whatever emotions and dark demons exist within them or within their interactions with others. Many simply repress those feelings, giving the appearance that all is well on the surface while retaining aggressions within their being or the need and desire to separate emotionally from others. This is what creates separation between people in marriages, relationships, and families, and results in unhappiness in many forms.

Sun Bear

Infidelity means someone has not been truthful and has had other partners, usually secretly. If a relationship were approached as an open relationship, then it would not be called infidelity. However, mostly when people get together, they choose to be exclusive to each other forever. That is a good thing for most people, but that is often simply an institutionalized form of protecting each other from unnecessary jealousy and envy. It is an outer way to make people feel inward emotional security.

However, most people are not in one relationship their entire life. There are people who have serial relationships, one after another. Some people may seek multiple partners, either openly or secretly. There are also people who do have one relationship their whole life. Are the people who have one relationship their whole life more right than those who have multiple relationships? Are those who have dishonest multiple relationships dishonest because they fear the outcome if they were to be honest? Who knows?

The point is, if people promise to be with each other and then one or the other breaks that promise that may not be okay. But sooner or later, where there is hurt as a result of broken promises, it has got to be let go. That does not mean it has to be let go, accepted, and tolerated within the relationship. It means that the person who feels hurt must let go of that hurt in order to move on, which is what I mean by it has to be accepted.

Merlin

In some ways, all of you share a common state of being, and in some ways, you do not. There is a certain part of everyone's reality that overlaps, but is it really reality or is it your reality? For example, everyone might agree that the sky is blue, that the grass is green, and so on. However, if you really think about it, what is blue? It is an agreement, is it not? You agree to call something a particular color and other things by other colors. You have certain things you agree upon because it makes it simpler to function, does it not, when you have certain things upon which you agree? Nevertheless, the more things there are, the harder it is to agree.

For example, you all do not agree with exactly the same politics, exactly the same religion, exactly the same thoughts on spirituality, exactly the same points of view about relationships, and many other things. In general, you have a certain body of thinking that is culturally accepted. As an example, in your particular culture it generally is accepted that everybody can have one partner at a time. It is not culturally accepted to have more than one partner at a time. It is also culturally agreed upon, within a certain spectrum of consciousness, that it is better to be married or have been married than never to have been married.

There are certain amounts of cultural beliefs, but is it reality or is it just a mass agreement? How many of these agreements are forming your reality right now? How much of what you are holding onto as real is really real? Moreover, if it is not real and it is just agreement, is it relevant? What if it is not relevant, but you agree? What if all of these irrelevant agreements, except for the fact that they help you function together, are irrelevant in terms of reality, and suppose your agreements inspire aspirations you attempt to attain, but these things have nothing to do with anything.

This is what people are finding out time and time again, that the things they have been taught to aspire toward, if they are finally able to attain them, leave them feeling empty inside. I often hear things such things as, "Why is it that I cannot stand my beloved soul mate, which I was madly in love with when I got married? I cannot wait until they leave the house, and I hate it when they come home. I thought that I was supposed to have the love of my life. What happened? Ah, it might be the wrong person. Let me get rid of them and find another one."

What if it is all irrelevant? What if it does not matter and you have all just agreed that these things do matter? Maybe for a short amount of time you felt a little better when you had some successful intimacy. However, what does that have to do with the truth? What if all that was, was just a little companionship? What if that has nothing to do with the answer to your existence? It really does not.

We are so tickled when people come to us and say, "Who is my soul mate? When will I meet my soul mate? If only I had my partner, it would be so much easier. I just want somebody here at least to try to have a relationship with while I try to get the rest of my life together. It is better than having nobody."

Our answer is maybe it would make life easier, maybe not. It might be worse, even much worse. However, what if you really do not have a clue? How many of the things you hold as vital and real are really real? Seekers of truth must ban together and learn from each other's experiences. You must hear those who have walked before you, whether they come in other times or in your time, because, believe it or not, you can come to this world again and again and still not have a clue.

Sun Bear

Human beings of this world have been successful in some areas, but are not very far along when it comes to the areas of jealousy and envy. In fact, jealousy and envy bring out the worst in human beings, greed, murder, and avarice. It is necessary for human beings to get far beyond these things in order for their world to survive. Love is institutionalized to protect against the violent responses of jealousy and envy, and maybe that is a smart thing when a culture is at this point of development.

Merlin

If you are on a spiritual path, you are always going to have individually to work to maintain the level of your own spiritual consciousness at a level far beyond anything that will easily work with the populace at large. This is particularly true for those who are married or have relationships or who are seeking relationships. Since your interest is in your survival and the levels of struggle to survive are rather high, the need to end the matter of struggle for survival is predominantly your focus. It will rule your ability to notice a soul mate rather than another kind of mate who provides relative comfort to your survival. These two things are often confused.

Soul mate relationships are particularly extraordinary kinds of relationships. However, in no way do they work out for evolved spiritual souls in such ways as are harmonious with that that functions in the collective agreement. Instead soul mate relationships tend to work out in ways that are extraordinary and outside of the collective agreement, if the soul mates are evolving or evolved souls.

If the partners in soul mate relationships are not part of a higher order of evolution within their civilization, soul mates are easily found. However, the moment you begin to evolve and are in contact with a higher level of consciousness and with a higher level of beings, the matter of soul mate and partnership becomes an extraordinarily challenging issue. This is why most people with an evolved consciousness are not with their soul mate as partners. They are with their soul mates in other ways, oftentimes as friends or temporary lovers and in many other forms, but not as life partners. It is rare to find soul mates as life partners. What will more often occur is that one partner in a long-term partner oriented relationship will evolve more than the other partner, which is not to say that evolution is better or somehow more vital.

Souls do not evolve in a graduated sort of way as in grade one, grade two, and so forth. If there were to be a thousand levels of learning, you may have lesson one, then lesson five hundred, then lesson two. Since you are nonlinear beings, you must work at the level that is available to you, capture, utilize, and cultivate that level through trust. This allows some people who have been working in a spiritual way for twenty years to come together with others who have been working spiritually only a few years. However, this does not mean they are at the same level of awareness or consciousness. It simply means they are getting the same teaching at that particular point in time. What is important to understand is that what is available to you, because it is there, is available for you to embrace and utilize if you wish.

Sun Bear

Not everybody comes to this earth for the purpose of marriage and having children. Those particular areas may not be the real places where a soul needs to develop or at a soul level one makes a choice about what is important because it is not possible to do everything. Therefore that soul chooses to express one part of themselves and not another. It is as simple as that.

Merlin

Old souls, in their need for survival throughout a number of incarnations, despite their wisdom, power, love, and inherent goodness, become extraordinarily self-centered. For lifetimes, they have struggled with their own survival, and they do not want anybody getting in their way. Hence, in relationships old souls tend to say to their partners things like, "You are holding me back," if they can even get a partner.

Old souls have a difficult time holding onto partners because their partners can hardly keep up with them, and usually think they are the most arrogant and selfish people. The old soul would say, "Who me? I am the most loving, giving person you will ever meet. You will never find another like me." That is true, so they do not have any idea why their partner would say anything like that about them. But an old soul is often in a desperate grab for survival, and they may not realize how focused they have become on themselves in their search for psychic survival.

The struggle for survival is why old souls cannot stay in contact with the Infinite. They may have moments of contact, but one can only remain in contact with the Infinite if the purpose is unselfish and honest. Therefore, an old soul will only find fulfillment when they are giving away what they love to give to those who need or want it. That is when the old soul knows the meaning of God, service, and happiness. To give like that is an extraordinary challenge because the old soul has also become quite powerful and can be a bit controlling. That is what was said to me when I was an old soul a long time ago. In fact, I think I was born old.

The old soul oftentimes has to have everything just the way they want it, and may not even realize that demand. If an old soul loves tidiness, then everything must be in its place. However, most old souls do not love tidiness, instead loving their particular organized mess. Let anybody disturb that and it will insight the rage of an old soul. Do not touch their mess or move anything around because the old soul is trying desperately to hold their world in place by carefully arranging everything and after endless incarnations, everything is finally just the way they want it, so do not dare disturb it.

The old soul must become open to new ideas, and this is hard. They must seek to be open-minded and seek to be giving. The giving part, to an old soul, feels like being a slave because they have issues about others taking advantage of them. They remember days when they were used for everyone else's ends, and now feel in charge a little bit. They feel they are in their own expression of why they are here, an opportunity for which they have longed. However, after a while old souls can see that, despite their inherent beauty, wisdom, and goodness, they also have their own character flaws, and they are usually very aware of them. They are usually very hard on themselves about their flaws and need to learn how to love themselves in a gentle and easygoing manner.

The more self-love an old soul has the more a strange thing begins to occur. A loving fellowship begins to build up around them as they meet other likeminded old souls and recognize each other right away. When old souls meet each other, they must help one another. They must begin to put down their walls, because your fellows are sent to you with a purpose, holding the keys to cause your life to become more fulfilled and happier.

Old souls want to receive their well-being magically, graciously, soulfully, and meaningfully, otherwise they have little tolerance for making it happen on their own. Every now and then, when they get desperate enough from having nothing, they will try to force themselves into some position in life that is supposed to cause them to achieve enough resources. This may be done by putting themselves in a relationship to benefit from the support of a partner or through a job or schooling and many other things of this nature. Not that these things should not be done, but old souls have little tolerance for them. If their outcome is a desire for survival, but their heart is not in it, an old soul will begin something and drop out a thousand times in a thousand areas.

It is spiritual instinct for an old soul to want to find their path, but they must be active toward finding it. Part of that activity is, believe it or not, prayer and seeking communion with the Infinite Resource. This is essential, otherwise all the old soul will have is an insane mind that is constantly coming up with plans that do not work or they will not have the strength of their own will and the power will run out before they get to their willful goals. Old souls must have contact with the Infinite Resource and communion with it frequently. They must mediate, pray, dialog, and commune with the invisible. The prayer of an old soul is something like this. Help me to be of service to others. Let my motives increasingly become of the Spirit. Let me lose my fear of life, other people, and personal concerns. Let me embrace my well-being and the well-being of all. Let me help, even as I seek others to be helpful to me.

Increasingly old souls must seek this holy and sacred union, for that is the only source of power for an old soul. If they are still mad at the Creator, they must ask Creator's help to remove that because they cannot afford anger. It is all right to be angry, but the problem really is that they are hurt and scared, not angry. That is the truth. They are scared and hurt because of the underlying fear that they will not make it and will die because they do not have any power. That is the truth of what is going on.

Philos

What you think of as love might not really be love. When we speak of love, we speak of the very power that is life and eternity. Those possessed of this quality of love tend to manifest conditions of being that enable them to let go of a great deal, and therefore are more successful in negotiating their survival. Those not possessed of this quality of love become less connected to an eternal or higher level of functional nature and use other modalities to survive such as survival of the fittest. Love is really a power that generates life more and more successfully at different levels and ultimately becomes eternal.

For human beings at this stage the most balanced love is a love that is unconditional and without limit. This is a tall order for most human beings, for there is no reason to love unconditionally. There is every reason to love conditionally to promote survival. Indeed, conditional love allows a being to sort out what is useful and what is harmful to their more self-centered motivations, which are always toward survival with 'me first'. This attitude often is thought to reflection a healthy psychology.

Spiritual awareness though, at its highest level, is the antagonist of a healthy psychology because it is not putting oneself first. However, if a being is to survive, they must put themselves first at some point. It is healthy, and a being must orchestrate this successfully until they glean the necessary understanding for life at a different level of consciousness. If a being does not do this first, then the spiritual reality will utterly dissipate and destroy them, leaving no possibility for the eternal nature.

Merlin

Love is a power that people often get confused with an emotion. For example, if you were in the presence of a soul mate, you may feel incredible feelings of well-being, love, attraction, connection, support, and psychic opening, which are feelings tied into the emotions. These feelings can come and go, but they are not love. Love may produce these feelings. Love is the source of these feelings. Love is the power in whose presence you may feel some of those things. Equally, in the presence of love some people may not feel these things. Some people may feel fear, and in the presence of fear some people may want to close down, run away or shut off in the presence of what is really love.

Love is the power, not the feeling, and is only useful to anyone when it is in action. For example, take the idea of love in the form of a relationship. Because love can be expressed in many forms, you can be with someone with whom there is a feeling of love as well as the presence of the power of love. However, at a particular point in time love may ask something of you that you do not want to give, and it is different for each person. The presence of the power of love may cause someone to want to be in a committed relationship, which for another person is the antithesis of love.

Let us say that one person arrives at a point in their life where they may no longer want a number of different partners and instead they want only one partner. They fall in love with someone, but they are not habituated into the idea of having one partner, even though they want only one partner. Sooner or later it comes to the point where their fear causes them to feel that they are trapped and they do not want to be trapped in a relationship. Or it may be that they feel overpowered by the relationship or something of that kind, yet they may truly love the person with whom they are in relationship.

In this instance, because the motive was the desire to give and have some love in their life, they have to confront their fear of being in a committed relationship. They have arrived at a point where the power of love has moved them such that they may want to face their fears, so then they must act. That is love in action. The love is expressed through actions, which reflects commitment in this instance. They may also walk away from a committed relationship, feeling just as much love, deciding they cannot do it. The love is there, but they may not be able to express it toward another through acts of commitment. They may have to express their love through commitment at a later time when they are more able.

Love through commitment could be good if it is expressed to that person whom they love, because that person whom they love is given to or healed by that commitment. The person giving the commitment may also then grow by that commitment. Equally, they may do some good, if they are not able to commit, by letting go of that relationship and committing themselves in other ways that are important for them to commit. Good also is produced in that way.

Taking another example, let us say that person who is at the point of love and commitment really does feel some love for another person and cannot commit. Instead, they try to manipulate the relationship so that they can derive their needs from it without really loving. They may try to control getting their need met from the other person without surrendering to what love is. To me that is evil. It is destructive. It is harmful. Or, for example, let us say that the person at the point of love fails to recognize that they cannot or do not want to or shall not commit at that time, but decides they want to blame the other person, making it the other person's problem. They begin to berate the other person and start to pull away, never facing the fact that they are the one who is afraid. That is evil and destructive and has karma attached to it. That kind of blindness creates consequences the blaming person shall have to live out.

Evil in this instance means the lack of self-reflection, self-honesty, and integrity, which in action creates consequences that produce harm for oneself and others. Evil of this kind, where possible, must be stamped out. It is stamped out through enlightenment, revelation, education, and awakening. Never is it stamped out through condemnation or judgment. It is very important to contribute to the good. One of the greatest reasons for coming into this world is to awaken and cause other suffering souls to awaken. That is a very important part of coming here.

Sun Bear

You were born because there is a Spirit of the Universe who wanted to love you and wanted to experience you experiencing the Spirit. The Spirit of the Universe wanted you to know love.

Merlin

Old souls do not always really find lovers, but instead they take hostages. They tend to draw in people whom they demand serve them. The old soul will expect the person they draw in to be exactly what they want them to be or they will have 'discussions' and 'arrange' things so that the other person is exactly as they want them to be. But sooner or later the old soul finds out this does not work.

The older the soul, the less it works. So they either give up on relationship altogether or they find someone they do not realize has taken them hostage while they were thinking they had taking the other hostage. This creates tension in the relationship and they eventually get rid of the partner. Usually they say things like, "I do not need this. All women/men are terrible. Just give me a servant, a lover now and then, and perhaps some money. I am not going to saddle myself with any permanent partnership of any kind."

Old souls tend to be tired in their spirits. Often, if they are in any partnership, it will look to outsiders as though one partner is being done a great favor by the other, which is a symptom of the hostage taking. Nevertheless, it does not really end there. Sooner or later the old soul contacts a profound, unquenchable pain, if they are paying any attention at all. That pain is their teacher and their salvation. It shall always be so. But what is the pain?

First, to resolve the pain the old soul must stop looking for the quick fix, the easy way out, the fast way to make money, the best relationship, their perfect person. The reason they must stop looking for the quick fix is that when they see others have what they want, often it does not occur to the old soul that the person worked for what they have. The old soul just refused to work for things, thinking it is beneath them to be a 'worker bee'. They are convinced they can find an easier way through.

Quite often, the old soul cannot tolerate hard, tedious work because they have been here too long for any of that. But the old soul must become humble enough to be a 'worker bee', if that is what it takes, because sometimes the beginning of the older soul loving themselves has to do, on some level, with them feeling good about what they are able to do. The older soul must sometimes set up small successes to be achieved so that they can have a good feeling about being successful with small things. This is very important.

The old soul must set up small ways to be a little successful about their health, about their spirituality, and about their work. They must stop with their grandiose dreams because those dreams are not for old souls, but are for the younger souls. The old souls will never achieve a grand dream by holding the grand dream because when little faltering things happen along their way to the grand dream they will get so depressed that they think they are worthless. Therefore, the old soul must be humble enough to see a smaller distance. They must be self-reflecting, asking themselves, "Where, throughout my life, despite my soul searching, has all of my manipulation left me with a weak character?"

The old soul must be willing to develop their character. If they think they have done that, they are blind because old souls need daily to look at themselves saying, "Could I have done somewhat better today? Was it really that other person's fault in that circumstance? Is everybody really that stupid? Is it really that everybody just does not get it and that is why they do not do it my way? Is my partner really as frustrating as I think they are? Am I really all that bad too? Can I really be so terrible?"

The old soul's thoughts can range from "I am the best and everybody else is terrible," to "I am the worst and everybody else is great." They tend to go between these extremes with questions like, "Am I not just one more soul living in the world? Could I really have been that bad? Is it not all right just to be an average human being? If I am just an average human being, do I not have room to do a little better? If that is true, where do I get the power to do a little better?"

The old soul is usually frustrated because they do not know how to do better. Nevertheless, maybe that is what spirituality is all about, the seeking of the Source to get the power to do a little better than you had the power to do on your own. Maybe spirituality is about being more loving toward yourself than you otherwise had the power to do.

Sun Bear

It is new in your culture for women to be educated, empowered, and to have careers instead of being thought of as chattel. In addition, there is no traditional teaching for men to accept this new role of women. Therefore, many times men get married with one idea, even if they say something else, and women get married with another idea, which is not necessarily in alignment with the man's idea. However, culturally it is mostly men who have some difficulty adjusting to non-traditional women, even those men who say they have room for the woman to grow as she wants.

Ultimately, what is happening in your era is something greater than what people focus on in individual relationships either culturally or globally. Many people who did not have power are beginning to claim power, and those who formerly held the power may not always want to share it. This is happening all over the world in all kinds of circumstances and situations. As it was always a minority who held the power and not a majority, the people without power are in far greater numbers and are going to claim some of the power for themselves. This will cause old institutionalized structures to be redesigned, which includes relationships.

The result of the changes in the power structures of the world is that many women are leaving relationships like marriage because it no longer can contain them. In addition, the women who are married and who have successful careers often think they are not doing justice to their children. There is incredible guilt in women about their children when it comes to being successful in the world because rarely are the fathers available for parenting.

It is really going to be up to men and women to prepare their children for a broader kind of love, broader kind of support, and broader kind of relationship. Increasingly there will have to be more kinds of relationships because love must expand beyond ownership and power structures that limit one or the other of the partners. Relationships are going to have to take new forms, which will take many more generations to develop.

What is affecting relationships more than anything else is now has very little to do with individuals not being able to get along. It is a movement taking place at the level of the culture being guided by the need for human beings to grow and expand beyond limited ways of living and loving. The high divorce rate, seen by some as a negative sign of the times, is really a necessary transition from one place in your culture to another place in your culture that is less limiting to the individual. It is simply that things cannot change and remain the same. It is one or the other, not both.

Merlin

What kind of beings are you really? How much of who you are can you truly understand by simply trying to survive from one day to the next? Do you ponder these things? How will you ever discover anything about these things if you do not think about them? How will you get anywhere? How will you find out the truth unless you make time for the truth?

The little forms of relief you have from time to time are not enough. For example, finally having found your partner after searching for so long may be an incredible relief that you appreciate for a short time. However, has that ever been the answer? For instance, before you know it, you find out that you and your partner have issues. That is not something you wanted. You wanted so desperately for your partner to be the answer, but they could not be the answer. Even though they are a tremendous, beautiful relief to your instinctual search, you found you needed more than mere relief.

Not realizing they need more than the instinctual relief of companionship, a dilemma is created as a being keeps looking for companionship to be something it shall never be. That is very painful. In fact, it is so painful and karmic for some that they keep coming and going from relationship to relationship looking for the right one. They think the relief they will one day find will be the answer to their life. They may not think that consciously, but that is what they are secretly hoping.

Maybe if you are alone and see someone else with a partner, you think that person has found an answer that you have not. The same is true with work and money, physical well-being, security, and your place within your society amongst your peers. All of these things are just the human animal part of your nature for which you are trying to provide. They are instinctual demands for your survival, which you must provide for either as individuals or collectively as a species. It is the species instinct.

The species cannot survive unless it is a society because no individual can make it by himself or herself, not without an inter-special relationship. Every species must have a culture to live amidst so the species can have some longevity. The instinctual needs are therefore instincts of your species and not great spiritual callings.

When you want a lover or when you want to have sex it is an instinct of the species that is built into you. When you want to have job security and you want a house and a piece of land, those things are instincts to be safe in your person. That is an instinct you have as a human animal to be safe in your person. The fulfillment of the instincts of your species, the animal instincts, is relieved by the attainment of certain things, but that is not spirituality. That compensation can never fulfill the soul. Security will not fulfill your soul. Relationship will not fulfill your soul. Recognition by your peers will not fulfill your soul. The satisfaction you legitimately feel does relieve your instincts and is vital, but that is not the same as fulfillment of your soul. Fulfillment of the soul is something different.

What addresses your soul? The answer is the spiritual experience, and that is the last thing for which an old soul will look, even though there is nowhere else they can go. The old soul must go directly to the Source of Existence for all of their answers. Even though many old souls know this, they do not do this.

Isis, Miriam and Quan Yin

Your life is a gift. It is up to you to discover why and what you may further do with the life you have been given. The key to that discovery is love. You must find and hold love, letting it become powerful in your spirit. It is up to those who seek love and find love to bathe in it, allowing themselves to be transmuted, transformed by that love until their spirit is filled with power and light.

There is much you shall easily misunderstand while earnestly and sincerely seeking to embrace the light of love. You will, from time to time, be confused or misinterpret what you think you understand. Nevertheless, continue to seek and find the love, allowing yourself to receive the guidance that comes from the love that will awaken your spirit.

Your dedication and commitment to truth and love must come from deep within your own spirit after having had revelation. That is to say, after you have touched some spirit of the light and awakened some love, some understanding, some truth, and some awareness of the gentle spirit deep within your innermost nature, it shall necessarily fall to you to cultivate your character to be strong in the ways of light, giving up much to embrace much, much more. The tendency to be distracted by many diversions, many petty desires, and many strong instinctual draws will pull at your spirit. You must find your focus amidst everything. It is not hard to find your focus provided you are willing also to gradually let go of all old idea and notions of who you thought you were and who you expect yourself to be.

You must hold certain expectations, if the expectations you hold are shaped by the Spirit of the Divine. What those expectations are, you must come to understand. You must have the courage to see, to gain some notion, to embrace trail and error, and to forgive yourself and others, and then the spirit of light and of love will attend you. If you are unwilling to let go of much that is demanded that you let go, you shall be confronted by your own desire for spiritual awakening and your desire to resist spiritual awakening. Sooner or later you will see what you need to let go so that you may advance deeply and more powerfully into the spirit of truth.

The journey for each person is deeply personal. No one finds it easy all of the time. You are embracing a nature that holds no limits, but those limitless dimensions of being are not yours for the asking to simply use in such ways as are petty distractions of your ego. Much strength and discipline is necessary on this journey.

You will find that you must let the Spirit of the Divine shape and even discipline your character. By this, we do not mean that you are punished or beaten by the Divine. Rather we mean that the times will come, again and again, where you shall have no choice but to embrace the highest principles of truth available to you. Otherwise, you will suffer terrible confusion because of a desire to impose what you want on life rather than embrace what life would try to reveal to you.

Therefore, we beseech you to approach your life with an exceedingly open mind and a humble heart. Have the willingness to face and let go of personal designs upon your life and destiny if that is revealed at a certain time by your sincere search for truth. Your personal designs must be let go to be reshaped.

Your practice must become a daily seeking of higher guidance, asking for divine awakening to point out the best approaches to your life. You must ask to be freed from the egoistic demands of self-centeredness, selfishness, and fear. When these things come upon you, you must recognize that as a time when you need the help of the Divine rather than feeling justified by the instinctual responses for fear and self-centeredness that you find so easily.

It is important to recognize these dimensions of instinctual response in your being as the shadows that block the true path from your vision. The wiser the soul the more that soul asks to be lifted above these sentiments so that a clear path may stand revealed and the way of the power of light and truth, which is love, may flow into your heart and mind.

The time comes when all that had been of importance to you in the temporal world has gradually been taken away and you find yourself still existing, still possessed of the gift of life, spiritual consciousness, energy, and will. Soon it becomes apparent that the energy, life, and will are meant to flow in a particular direction that makes life and existence rewarding. Such a soul continues their journey and becomes familiar in the ways of love.

If you are such a soul, who has found these things to be true, we congratulate you and welcome you onward. If you have not found those things to be true, we welcome you onward and alert you to a higher path while making ourselves in the realm of Spirit available, if you should wish the journey.

No souls, having embraced the path of power, light, and love becomes perfect. No matter how shaped by the Divine that being becomes, how surrendered into Divine will, that being shall never become flawless in their choices and free of error. Do not therefore seek perfection, for that is simply the demand of the ego nature, which demands perfection from fear of making mistake or need for adulation, approval, and acknowledgement. Leave all of those ways behind, but know some of those ways will pursue you until your last days. It is there where the quality of forgiveness is necessary, for you will have to forgive yourself for where you are not perfect and be tolerant and forgiving of others, for they too shall be imperfect.

As you continue your journey the Supreme Divine shall continue to make revelations of the most simple and beautiful kind in your life from day to day. The gifts of life are endless, and since there is no difference between the inner and the outer dimensions, the gifts of the Divine shall flow to you from every quarter, seemingly inwardly and outwardly. Yet this flows most potently to those souls who would seek the real meaning of their existence and whose intention is to be useful to humankind and to the Supreme.

Sun Bear

You can come to know and love somebody by hearing their soul and knowing this is their reality. You can go into the reality of another and be with them in their reality and share their life and share love right there in the core of their understanding. It is as simple as being willing to listen.

Merlin

The soul has pretty much one need, which is love. Nothing feeds the soul better than love. The trouble is that sometimes a person approaches love through wanting love, and love is a very hard thing to define. The power of love is felt when a human being gives something through their actions. That is what taps a person into love. The state of energy that is the power of love can be connected to in meditation or through touching somebody who can contact the feeling of the energy state that is the power of love, but can only be sustained through giving. A soul needs to give.

The trouble is that the human psyche wants to get when it needs to give. A human being does not give for very long before the human psyche starts thinking about what it can get, and will stop giving until it starts getting. Since that make sense to the soul, it starts wanting and needing. In other words, if you stop giving because your psyche or personality self talks you into not giving, that causes you to starve on a soul level. You are going to start wanting, and you are going to start trying to manipulate contracts.

Some people can get away with that for a very long time because they are very good manipulators. They can invent all kinds of contracts that they think are serving their soul's needs. There are books written on manipulation to get what you want. They are wonderful psychological treatises on corporations and compromises and all of these sorts of things. That all sort of works on the personality level and may be very satisfying to some people. However, the soul needs to give. If left to the soul, the soul would give all of the time.

Love, which is the soul's need, when it comes to people, is really one hundred percent one-sided. That means all you can do is give love and forget about everything else. If love is not one hundred percent one-sided, there is something else going on. And if you are giving when you do not have it to give, then that is not giving, but instead is sacrifice. Nobody likes to be sacrificed.

To give to others you must first find something rich within yourself. From this place within yourself all manner of love will begin to come to you in all manner of directions. Sometimes love does not come romantically, but comes instead through friendship, through support, through experience and learning. You are enriched by your giving, and that enrichment also nurtures your soul. That is love.

You cannot always control when you are giving or to whom you are giving because the fact is, when you give in whatever ways you are able to give your soul's essential need begins to manifest. That is not what you want, but what you need begins to manifest, which may also be what you want, but that depends upon how awake you are. Therefore, when you give your soul is being enriched and you are added to in the ways you need.

Sometimes you may give for years in the way that is natural for you to give before you start to feel full. This is because you may have your 'I' or your psyche attuned to what you want while your heart is giving what you need to give. You may feel you never get what you want, but you must just keep on giving what your soul loves to give. This could lead to misery because while you are giving what you need to give one hundred percent, your mind may be attuned to what you want, which might be zero percent happening. That is all right because even though what you want to be happening is not happening, your soul is being nurtured on some level even while your mind is miserable.

Sooner or later you will have an awakening at the soulful level that takes you past your mental breakdown, the breakdown that has happened because you never got what you wanted. Then suddenly you begin to feel as though you receive endless reward. This change in perception is because all the while behind your back your soul has been being nurtured, even while your mind or personality self has felt it has been starving. Usually it is not that extreme. How it usually works is that if you are giving from your soul, you are satisfied in your personality sense in some ways here and there, sometimes even in great ways. But sooner or later, if soulful giving takes place, there will be a rich response because you will have been creating that destiny with your soulful giving.

The soul needs love. That is its only need, love. Interestingly enough that love is about giving, which is the only way. Love is not a state of being. It is a power that comes through actions, usually actions of giving, and that is what the power of love is all about, giving. Love takes you beyond or out of the false self and into the real self. You can tap into the state that is love in your meditations. The energy state and/or emotion of overwhelming feelings of beauty are a cognizance of a piece of what love is. However, the power of love only grows strong as you express it, as you give it, and that is what the soul needs to do.

Sun Bear

There are places inside of everyone that are really very sick, usually around the matter of love. This is true for everyone. Sick means more than twisted up inside. It is the inability to love. In fact, so ill are some at times that all one is able to do is let a little love come in to them, a very, very little bit, and is not really able to give love. This does not mean kindness, affection, and compassion. It is a kind of love or giving where there is really no expectation of something in return. To love like that is extremely difficult for some. The idea that many have is that when they give their heart in its most open way the other person better well return it. That is just how vulnerable this place inside is, how ill this place is from lack of love. Therefore, the sickness is really the lack of love, and some are just that ill from not having love.

Therefore, upon meeting the Great Spirit, even in the form of a lover, a great deal of this illness shows up. However, Great Spirit can handle it, and the only thing you really can do is say that for right now you can love, for right now. Tomorrow you may not be able to love. Ten minutes ago, you might have been in another state of mind, but right now, it is about love. The love had to be very much in the present moment. Real love is such a power that the lack of it makes people feel sick. In the presence of the opportunity to love and be loved a lot of sickness will show itself. However, a little love can also be present.

Merlin

Love, insofar as relationship is concerned, may best be described as devotion, giving your time and energy. That is giving your time and energy, not getting it, but giving it. If you can give your time, energy, and focus and not sacrifice it, you are giving love to your partner. If you discover that your partner is giving you attention, devotion, time, and effort, you are being loved.

However, it is also very possible to have a partnership based on needs being met on a basic human physical level that is missing devotion. Therefore it is important to know the difference between love and devotion and having your needs met. When you are truly giving your love and devotion, you never have to worry about that giving. Even if nothing is being given in return, if you have that clearly separated from what are you needs, you will never have to worry. When you find yourself in total enjoyment of giving it is likely because you are also being given to in kind.

Devorah, Olga, Helga (the Sisters Three)

There are many keys, but perhaps the strongest key to everything in this dimension is relationship, and presumably successful relationship. We do not necessarily mean romantic relationship, but all kinds of relationships are vital to existence here. You will not get off as easily as saying things like, "Oh, these men (women, family, groups, institution), I can't stand them. Who needs them?" That does not work. You do not get out of this dimension like that. Instead, you must orient yourself toward serving. That is the only way any relationship can work, with an attitude of giving, of being helpful. If you want to be much less successful at relationship, simply orient yourself toward, "How can I get what I want?"

When I, Devorah was here, I had a little bit of a challenge getting on intimately with men. Then I discovered just how I was going to do it, and I was so liberated. It was my last incarnation here, and I found this was the single thing that helped me finally let go and go elsewhere. That is not to imply that you incarnate here for the purpose of trying to get out, because you do not. However, my formula was a very simple one. I decided I did not need to saddle myself with any man. I just thought I would have lots of money, find a little bit of service, hirer a servant, and take a lover now and then. What a beautiful formula that was, and I recommend that path for those of you who can do it. It will not work for everyone because there are those of you who have other business here and you will be about that business. That is how I did it because it could not work out for me any other way.

Relationships are very vital. You have to live amidst them, and if you can find enough love, then you can really, really live. The greatest power that you will come to find is love. It is a very strange power though, because love is not something that is always particularly sweet. Love attempts to be elegant, noble, and kind, but is not necessarily always sweet. Love attempts to be affectionate, supportive, and truthful, but it is not always sweet. Love is usually forgiving, and can be equally exacting as well because the love of which we speak is not really an emotion.

There are many emotions associated with love because love awakens lots of emotions. However, love can also awaken emotions that have little to do with love. Those emotions can also be felt when there is the presence of no love. Love can stimulate lots of feelings, but those feelings are not necessarily the same as love. Love is a power that sources, at its root, just about everything, but not everything necessarily is love.

Someone who is possessed of sufficient love eventually becomes powerful enough to live and be full, no matter where they are and no matter in what dimension they exist. That is a great part of what you learn in relationship. One of the keys to a great part of the formula of love is tolerance, tolerance, tolerance. The tolerance of which I speak is not necessarily agreement. In fact, sometimes love requires embracing things or allowing to exist things that are in direct opposition to your beliefs and understandings. You will have your own specific things that are like this and each person is different, but tolerance is absolutely required.

In relationship, where there is love, if you find sufficient love to allow and you have tolerance, you will also be supported and benefited by much that comes from those for whom you have tolerance. The difficulty in relationship is that sometimes you will think you really need agreement in order to love. At times, you will feel agreement and love are synonymous. However, there are circumstances and principles where you can be diametrically opposed to each other and still hold the power of love.

Intimacy is the most powerful teacher, and you need to have very powerful intimate relationships that will provide for you in some form or another. Powerful intimate relationships may not always come in the form of romantically oriented relationships, but may come in the form of a relationship with your art, a career, a convention or an institution or with a lover. However, the intimacy, the depth of profound communion and involvement will be necessary in order to cultivate the power that is love.

Think for a moment about the lengths you may have gone to in extending love and tolerance to those for whom you care. How much have you learned about yourself in doing that? Think about how often you have been surprised in unsuspected ways, how much you have learned from those who are different than you. That is very, very important.

Sometimes people believe they must align themselves with people like themselves. That is the natural instinct of just about everyone on this planet. However, even though that is the natural instinct, nobody can come into this world and do that, and get away with it. Sooner or later everyone is introduced to and must make peace with things, values, people, and circumstances that are very different than they are. This is a way of expanding.

Eventually you come to a point where you say, "How did I, with all of my thoughtfulness, high spiritual development, and intellectual awareness, wind up in such a circumstance as this with these children (parents, business partner or love relationship)? How did I ever get this way?" No matter how hard you try, no matter how much you think you learn, no matter how much you swear you will never do it this way again, you seem to always wind up at this point again and again. No matter how discriminating you are there always seems to be certain things that creep in at the levels closest to you and grab you unaware. Is that something wrong or simply the nature of how growth is promoted? Can you make it any easier? Yes, you can. How can you make it easier? Make it simpler. Do not worry about ease, because you might not be able to have it easy. However, you can make your existence relatively simpler.

Some people have very funny notions about what loving themselves means. Some people associate it with giving themselves everything they want. Can you imagine that? Why do people associate loving themselves with giving themselves everything they want? Giving yourself everything you want is not the equivalent of loving yourself. Try giving yourself everything you want. First, can you even figure out what you want? Moreover, if you do figure out what you want, just set out on the road to getting it and you will learn much. Sooner or later you will come to the conclusion that everything you want really is not all that important. It may not be the conclusion you come to before you set out to get everything you want, but sooner or later you will come to that conclusion.

Some people are afraid to make a few things important. They think, "Well, what about all those other things? If I make a few things important, those other thing that I want might get by me. What about all the other things out there that I will miss?"

You must be careful of this kind of thinking. Instead, just go ahead and set out to get what you want. Making your life simpler means simplifying some of what you want. If you are very appreciative of what you claim and what comes to you that you feel you want, you will be ever so happy, but you must remember to be appreciative of it.

A tremendous power to claim your existence in a strong, healthy, loving, and profound manner has much to do with letting things be simpler and letting go more. It is not really so much about claiming. In fact, you may even find that to claim too much, whatever too much is to you, is so far from loving yourself that it is sometimes almost the opposite. Claiming too much can be very abusive to you. For example, have you ever found that to be true with food? Perhaps you have found it to be true with sex or maybe with pleasure of any kind. Things that are delightful, when overdone, become very difficult and painful and often have terrible consequences. So giving yourself whatever you want may not be the same as loving yourself or the same as nurture.

The next time you find yourself letting go of some things so that you can embrace what is simply more important to you, maybe you will remember our affirming message about the safety in doing that. If you can do that, you are really on the road to happiness and real fulfillment. The art of letting go is everything in your spiritual awakening. Nothing teaches that like relationships of all kinds.

Sun Bear

People want to be married because they want to be loved, but they also need security. Within that context, they can learn new things, if they are open.

Merlin

You may not realize it, but the Creator is a supreme lover. Moreover, many of you would think of the Creator as codependent because the Creator is a great 'yes' being. Whatever you ask from the deepest part of your core, it is just "Yes my child." For example, if you say "I will never have anyone," the Creator says, "Yes my child." If you say, "I could really need someone," the Creator responds, "Yes my child." The Creator responds to whatever is in your core.

Why would the Creator ever respond that way to a wounded soul? It is because the Creator has no fear, knows that all things eventually work out, and that love is the answer. So Creator just loves in an unconditional, extremely permissive way. In addition, we intervene many times on your behalf, pleading and begging with the Source of Existence not to bestow upon you some of the things you are asking for, because we know what you will go through if you get some of those things. However, there are times we cannot intervene because you do not know all of the time the level of the wounding that caused you to ask for what you believe you need.

You may be the most sick, insane, jealous, revengeful person that thinks all you really need is one really true woman in your life to really adore, love, and worship you and you would be fine. But sooner or later that woman does not respond in the way you need her to respond and your own wounding, which is very strong, asserts and somebody ends up in a great deal of pain or dead.

Another example would be someone who with such great, terrible and awful money problems who thinks that if they win the Lotto it would be a little easier. Then perhaps some money comes along and the first thing you know, because of lack of self-love, which probably got them into that desperate situation in the first place, they destroy themselves with all manner of self-destructive habits funded by the newfound money.

Some of you are absolutely convinced you know what will fulfill you and must search out every single option in every single place. You must satisfy yourself. That is a part of what lifetimes are for, satisfying yourself that all those things that you think work really do not work. You may have to do that life after life until you have explored every avenue and are convinced. However, you will come to a point where you realize that within your heart and consciousness is an access point to commune directly with the Source of Existence and, from that communion, to be guided. Even having the experience of communion may not be enough to make it the priority in your life, so you must explore all of the ramifications and versions of that.

Then there are those who think that because they are exploring every avenue and option to convince themselves this means they are terrible and awful and that the Creator is everything and they are nothing. That is not true either. Creator is beautiful and you are beautiful. When you feel separated from the Creator it is horrible for you and for the Creator, but together it is beautiful. When you are connected, you are happy and the Creator is happy. When you are not connected, the Creator is very unhappy, not angry, unhappy, and misses and wants you, loves and needs you to join with it.

The Creator is a longing lover, continually welcoming you. That is the Source. There are many manifestations of power in the universe, but unconditional love is the highest source, and it is the Creator you must seek and with whom to commune. Then you will begin to know the meaning of happiness. To the extent that you have connected with the Creator, you will know happiness. To the extent you have not connected, to that extent angst exists, calling you back again into union with Creator.

Philos

To simplify and give a kind of holographic impression we will say that there are particles of your soul that, in a sense, are broken off from you in this existence. These pieces are your soul parents, soul students, soul siblings, and other various levels of expression. There are also those with whom you mate or with whom you feel the need to integrate successfully totally and intimately. All of this takes place at a level of energetic impulse.

All of the time you are translating energetic impulses through your own vocabulary of ideas and principle so that you might say your understanding has many levels. One level of translation is an energetic namable or unnamable attraction or repulsion response that you understand or do not understand depending upon your ability clearly to articulate the energies you are receiving.

There are also particles of your soul that are in a sense broken off from your present incarnation and have gone into the light as well as ambient particles that have not yet incarnated. For better or worse, you are also connected to those particles.

Presumably, the particles that have gone into the light become your Guides at a point you do not know to be yourself. Those particles that have existed and not yet incarnated into this world or dimension, but shall incarnate, are your future soul connections at the level of soul parent, soul child, soul sibling, and soul mate, like those particles that are also now incarnate here.

This information may lead to a number of questions, but for now let us begin at the level of what we are calling soul mate. The soul mate is nothing more than a mechanical energetic attraction to a dimension of soul energy that has now split from some common larger whole and has expressed itself in more than one form, namely those who know themselves as soul mates. These soul mates may have more to do than simply be together for an eternity, which is a romantic projection of human beings and is not the case in truth.

Soul mate relationships are in fact very powerful, extraordinary relationships, but it does not mean you walk into the sunset with each other forever. It is better to say that if you have found a soul mate, be prepared to get down to business. You could not stay together in the first place at the level of soul and yet you are compelled to work it out. I will say that again. You could not stay together in the first place and yet you are compelled to work it out. That is a soul mate.

You cannot work things out with every soul attraction because not every soul attraction is a soul mate. It may be a vital soul attraction even when it is not a soul mate. Indeed, it may be every bit as vital as a soul mate, but it cannot be a soul mate if it is not a soul mate. It can only fulfill what it can be, which it is not a soul mate. It is whatever else it is, but it is not soul mate. You also cannot make a soul mate into anything but a soul mate, no matter how hard you try.

For example, a soul sibling is not a soul mate. In a way, all of these soul attractions are mated, but what we mean by soul mate is relative to your desire to walk into the sunset. A soul sibling is one with whom you may have a tremendous amount in common. Your parents may be like each other. You may think in similar ways. You may have gone through parallel life experiences. That is a soul sibling, not a soul mate. Very often soul mates do not have a parallel life experience, In fact, they are extraordinarily opposite from one another, which is why they have not figured out how to get along and yet feel compelled to be with each other.

A soul sibling is an enormous relief to find. Soul siblings are the ones who think just like you, who always support you, and you always support them. You just love them and they love you, although you may have rivalries sometimes with your soul siblings just like with any other siblings. Competitive rivalries may lead you to ban your soul sibling from your life for a while, and then they may return to your life. However, they are always soul family because you are united by a commonality on the journey.

A soul child is one toward whom there is an enormous attraction. Very often, there is a desire to protect them. In addition, more than anything else, there is receptivity to you on their part to learn from you. They make themselves available to you for learning at the level of a spiritual or professional path or any number of other things. A soul child is not necessarily the relationship between a guru and a disciple or a teacher and a student, but it is one where there is something to offer and something to be received whereby both beings find themselves happily functional in that position. In soul child relationships, one grows into them and out of them. Therefore, they are a more temporary kind of relationship. If it is a successful relationship, a permanent respect or love develops for the one who has soul parented the soul child.

Of course, sometimes, as with any form of relationship, things can go awry. The soul parent or soul child may want to hold on forever. The soul parent or soul child must know when to let go, and oftentimes neither knows how or when to do which. This is part of the learning experience of the soul parent and soul child.

The soul child cannot be a soul mate because there just is not enough there. Therefore, if a soul child is forced by some need to act as a soul mate, it will not work out in the same way that a soul mate relationship will work. It will more often than not lead to a disabling relationship for both the soul parent and soul child if it is forced to be something it is not.

Take, for example, the institution of marriage, a decidedly human institution. You may think that soul mate relationships can work out in a marriage, and they certainly can and often do work. The exception would be when, over the course of time, you have had many soul mates and your particular practice of the institution of marriage forbids communion with more than one soul mate. Then you have a conflict at the level of the soul, and there is something to be worked out, usually at a level that is more societal than individual, but that affects the individual. And what about the general moral principle that human beings have about singularity in relationship, whether or not it is the institution of marriage?

Therefore, you see, soul mate relationships do not necessarily fit the mandate of cultural norm. This is one of the ways in which, if you are attuned totally to yourself as a spiritual being at the expense of your human animal nature, you will set yourself at odds with the world around you.

Merlin

If you are not your body, then what exactly are you? How does what you are interact with your body? What is the purpose of your body relative to your soul and your spirit?

A quick answer might be that your body is an instrument through which you can learn, but let us look at this a little more closely. What exactly is the spirit? Is it a mystical, unfathomable, unnamable power that magically intertwines with the body? Is there actually a process of interaction that can be deduced in a linear, logical way? Can it be understood scientifically if you had the necessary instrumentation or devices to measure it?

People have tried to measure, notate, and categorize the spirit for many years, but it still has not been done in any universally provable manner. There are numerous keys that will start to unravel now that the genetic mapping has been completed, but naming the DNA does not mean you know its function. However, as this is slowly unraveled, you may begin to see how the DNA interacts with your body.

Many believe that the spirit is a sort of energetic system. But are you little electrical charges that zip and zap through your brain and body? If you think you are not your body, but you interact with your body, are you those little impulses that jump around in there? If you are, how do you know that? And if you are not, then who are you?

For many thousands of years some people have deduced there is at least one significant portal between the physiological body and the proposed spiritual body, which creates a tie between the cosmic and the mundane. These people believe this portal is in the lotus of the head, the seventh chakra near the pineal gland, and they are in fact correct.

The pineal gland secretes hormones, like serotonin, melatonin, and dopamine, which affect your state of mind. The secreted hormones tie into your entire glandular system, and the glandular system is connected to your chakras. And furthermore, the function of your physical and psychical body that effect you at the highest level of your spiritual, mental, and emotional function is your sexual organs, which may be surprising, but is pretty important.

Why are your spiritual centers connected to your sexual organs, as well as other organs in your body, and to the secretion of hormones? There is a message here that you are suppose to take as important. Why is it this way? Why is it important? If those things tie into each other, then just how do they tie into each other? How significant are they? If you learn about it, maybe the knowledge will free you from limitations and restrictions.

Sun Bear

Spirit always knows your heart, always loves you, and always accepts you just like you are right now. It does not matter how awesome you become or how small, you are always accepted by Spirit, because you are always just right.

Merlin

Creator is decidedly not impartial. The Creator loves and is favorable toward the humble because the humble are open to the Spirit flowing into them. They develop a relationship with the Creator, and the Creator favors them. The only thing the Creator does indiscriminately is give life, consciousness, to all, whether deserving or undeserving. However, if you want the favor of Creator, that takes humility. The humility that is needed starts with a simple prayer. "Help me. Show me. What would you have of me? Give me the power."

Sun Bear

You had better believe in the value of your own spiritual development because the world is not going to validate it for you. The world is not going to say, "If your spiritual value is true, then you should have a very nice house and the perfect soul mate." No, it is very likely that the world will make it hard in certain ways for you to address your needs. That is why so many come to us and say "I have this wonderful girlfriend. She is great. She is beautiful. But she just does not get me." What we will say to that, "So? Does she love you?"

You might say to us, "My husband (boyfriend), I love him so much. He is such a good man, but he does not understand me. He does not understand my path." We say, "So what? Who cares? Does he love you? Does he give to you? Is he there for you?" If you say yes, we do not see a problem.

The level at which a lover who loves you understands you does not require them to understand every element of your process. You should not even try to define, articulate, and reconstruct every element of their process either. That is the meaning of unconditional love. You do not need all of that, and can be in appreciation when you can love unconditionally. If you find yourself struggling at those levels of love, you must either let go or understand what got you together in the first place.

For example, maybe when you got together you really wanted a house, a family, and children. Maybe that was really important to you for reasons of fear and survival or maybe for reasons of love. Now you have gotten so high and you want something more. You have changed, but big deal, you grew.

However, you see there is something called karma. You set activity in motion that required you to be responsible longer than you expected. If you do not address it properly, it will come back and bite you. You had better take the right kind of attitude of consciousness and follow through with the nature of the way your human life is right now. You cannot successfully abandon your children because they do not understand you or abandon your parents because they do not get you. What about love and acceptance on both sides? That is the higher dimension of all of that.

There are all of these lessons you need to have here upon the earth. What about commitment? What about how can you love yourself and be committed when you really would rather not be because it is not suited to your current needs? This is a big one. That is all fine in non-spiritual terms, but if you are living a spiritual life, not everything is going to be suited to your needs at all times. You are going to have to open up your ability to give when things do not feel right. That is the meaning of being a sovereign being.

Merlin

Anyone who is intimate with another is hurt at some point by that other, whether an intimate sexual partner, soul mate or a family member. People who love each other also unintentionally and even intentionally hurt each other. A problem only develops when there is no forgiveness of self or other. Otherwise, if there were no forgiveness, you would be required to be perfect. Since no one is perfect, then it would be an awful, awful place. However, unconditional love does not mean you will never make a mistake. Unconditional means that you continue to love, sometimes through forgiveness, even when it is hard to continue to love. That is what unconditional means, without conditions. Everyone is, sooner or later, required to have this kind of love.

Azlo

Men and women are very good at fighting with each other and not good enough at loving each other. The problem is not competition, which is not unique to men, but is unique to humanity. Men are not imperfect and women more perfect, but there is an imbalance that is not due to competitiveness, which occurs in exactly the same way in female dominated societies. The imbalance is because human beings do not respect their minds sufficiently. They respect their bodies more than their minds, their property more than their minds and their possession more than their minds. Why is that? It is because men and women are interested in power, not love, and they do not know what to do with the power if they do not love. That is the problem. When human beings do not know how to love and they get hold of power, it drives them mad.

Sun Bear

Just because someone is your soul mate does not mean that they hold the same power as you. When a soul is with somebody who is much stronger, more powerful than they are, it is draining to the other person. Sometimes it happens between men and women. The man may be much more overpowering, much more overwhelming and may not justly use his power. You really cannot successfully be in a romantic relationship for a lifetime with someone you are more powerful than without great, great care.

I can think of many situations where the woman is so much more powerful than the man in the relationship. She wants her man to live up to this ideal that she sees in him, to his potential. He just will not do it, and she imagines herself as hurt, not given to. However, really what it is about is that she is far more powerful than he is. He is just not there yet. I have seen the opposite also where the man is so full of power that he sees a woman as despicable and weak. That can be so hurtful. It is very difficult to be with someone far more powerful than you are, even if it is a soul mate.

Soul mates are not perfect relationships. They just mean you are drawn together because you are either sympathetic or complimentary to each other. You can identify with each other, but you do not really have much or anything in common, even though you are compatible. It is like how the cogs of the wheel fit, but you do not always feel the same way. You can have love, but remember love is not an emotion.

Love is not dependent upon emotion. The power of love produces emotions. It produces hate. It produces warmth. Love is so powerful it can produce any type of emotion and is not dependent upon your feelings. Love produces feelings, for good or for ill, but love is not about happiness in relationship. Relationship is about getting things out of the way that stand in the way of love, and it is decidedly work at times and not happy work if you have lots of baggage.

Love is just like the Great Spirit. Great Spirit throws the romantic love at you first so that you can get a few hints at what you are in for with Great Spirit. If you can pass that test, you get Great Spirit. If you cannot, well Great Spirit will try to find another way to do it. Great Spirit can be like the vacuum cleaner salesman of the 1950's. They knocked on your door, and when you opened the door, they would throw some dirt into your house and then suck it up with the vacuum cleaner. Great Spirit is like that. Ding-dong. Hello. All nice at the door, then does something bad, asking to be let in to fix it for you, taking over everything to sell you something that you never expected. Then, when you are convinced, you buy it.

The thing is this. If you are fortunate enough to buy into it, you will be happy for the rest of your life. However, if you are too smart, you will not buy into it. You will think, "Wait a minute. Is this a little too manipulative? Who is this guy who came and barged in here and tried to sell me something? I never heard of him. Get out of here." However, if you are lucky enough to buy into it, Great Spirit may sell you a vacuum cleaner that changes your life.

La Compte de Sainte Germaine

The problem inherent in attracting your twin flame or soul mate may lay in the fact that you do not really believe it is possible to be loved by another who would accept you as you are. This belief takes years of training on your part to believe that you are unlovable. However, how could anything be further from the truth? How can you have that which your heart longs for if you do not think it is possible?

Remember, experiences of the past are not the future. There is a difference. Moreover, when you walk through life with the impression that you cannot have something, you repel that which you want with your very strong beliefs. You must instead find a way to change your thought patterns from negative and self-belittling to a more positive tone.

You must find ways to love yourself every day. It is vital that you feel nourished with peace if you want to attract your twin flame. Think of ways in which you are wrapped with peace, blessed, and graced. Dwell on your blessings until you truly feel them. Dwell on truly feeling blessed, for in this feeling is the experience of grace. Let your heart be that which longs for this union more than the mind and the body. In the heart lies the strength to attract such a love. Before you fall asleep at night, ask to be united with your love in the sleep state. Ask for this often. Calm your mind and ask for the experience of feeling loved before you fall asleep.

To attract a love that is special to you, you must follow principles of self-love. Pray to have grace enter your heart. This will attract more grace into your love life. Know that you would not be longing for this relationship unless it was possible. It is important to go through the feelings of longing. If not for the wanting, it would be difficult to appreciate a love so great.

Find peace within your heart, a time to not struggle with yourself, for if you do not do this, the new partner would only mirror these inner struggles. Therefore, be intimate with the longings within your own heart. Your heart, through its own wisdom, will lead you to your love. Look not so much outside of yourself to find your true love, but reach within. You must stretch for this love within. Alone you must seek and reach grace before it can be granted in your relationship.

Sun Bear

How many times have you heard about people who were in love, got married, and all of sudden everything changed and got terrible between them? What occurs for these people is that they have made significant commitments to choices that are part of a strong, powerful continuum beyond their previous unaware choices. They in fact become part of an entirely different reality than the one they left behind, which is confusing for them. They simply do not know where they are anymore or know the direction they are going. This sort of thing also happens when ordinary performers suddenly become famous or start to become wealthy. There is a disorientation and confusion that also occurs for these people.

People make choices that enter them into a new stream of life, a new place in the karmic continuum. Their choices do not change them, but change the conditions, circumstances, and things around them so much that they have trouble identifying with those elements. In fact, they go into a new dimension where their body is the same, the players are the same or appear to be the same, but there are new things to which they have never been introduced because it is an entirely different stream of life.

In fact, what happens is a person's consciousness has occupied a new position in an event called existence, but the soul, as it were, is still the same. There is simply an entirely new set of circumstances. It is a shifting stream that occurs within a lifetime as well as from lifetime to lifetime. From life to life, the bodies are sometimes similar to the bodies left behind, with similar appearance, affects, and patterns, but sometimes they are quite different.

What a person must do is remain committed to activating the new reality and not become confused by the strangeness of new appearances. This is done by holding to the original intention and not deciding there is somehow a faltering, because that will lead to becoming overwhelmed. Instead, there must be belief, knowing and acting in such ways as are harmonious with the new time stream of intention. That is in fact the meaning of 'to thine own self be true'.

Azlo

Both sensual and sexual education of your children is important, yet hardly exists in your culture. Of the two, sensual education is the most important. That is, to awaken your children's minds and bodies and to link sensuality with the mind is very important. Their senses must be free. The nose is meant to smell, eyes to see, nose to smell, mouth to taste, ears to hear, fingers to touch, and meditation to reflect. Meditations with eyes closed and open in beautiful environments are important.

With sexual education, teach much more than the functions of sex. Teach sensuality as well. This is very, very important for long life. Stop teaching children that sexuality is wrong and that their sexual organs are bad. That is horrible. Explain to children the purpose and use of the sexual organs and let your artists teach sensuality. They already lead the way.

Never be ashamed of your bodies or their nakedness, ever. Appreciate all of your senses. Teach children to have more and more freedom, but also teach them to be civilized within your culture. Most important, beyond education, you must teach children to respect the peace of others.

Merlin

Many people have misunderstood the allegory of Adam and Eve. First, who raised the world? Who are the ones who raised every single child? Of course, it was the women. Men are raised by women. Are those women conscious? Maybe those women are experienced in raising children according to the various cultures and traditions, and there is definitely love involved. However, I will go so far as to say that they are not conscious, absolutely not. Women would like to be conscious, but where would they get this consciousness? Would they get it from their mothers? Would they get it from their fathers? Where is the truth?

As far as the men are concerned, how do men feel about being raised by women, particularly when the women are not conscious? They are pissed off, resentful, and even hate it. They hate the women. As you can see, I am not mincing words here. Nevertheless, women need men and men need women. How do women feel about the men who resent them? They treat them like little boys. Yet those little boys go to their little mommies to be given what they want, a little sex, a little 'you did it right', and they hate the women.

What do men do when they hate women? They abuse women. They try to get control over women and humiliate them. What does a woman do who will not be humiliated? She defies men. Women, fueled with anger, try to defy their fathers and the men all around them, and what is a woman's power over a man? It is seduction. The battle goes on and on, women seducing men and men hating women.

What can you do about that when you get enlightened? If you are smart, not necessarily wise, but smart, you are going to opt out of the battle. Let it go. You are going to say, "Forget men (women). I am just going to take a lover now and then and just get what I want."

Men and women have an agreement. That agreement is "You give me a little sex and I will give you a little money. You give me a little love and I will give you a little security." It is an agreement, a negotiation. Moreover, your therapists buy right into the argument. They try to get everybody to compromise. Why? So that people can function. However, what does that have to do with the truth? Furthermore, when men and women get tired of their relationships the therapist tells them to get divorced, saying things like "Why are you in a relationship? You are not getting what you want. Get a relationship where you get what you want."

With this battle going on how would a woman get the love she wants? How is she going to get love when she hates her father and why would she hate her father? She would hate him because her father hated her mother and perhaps he even tried to seduce the little girl. Perhaps, since the father could not get what he wanted from his wife, maybe he wanted to get it from the little child. Maybe the little child wanted to give it to get the love from the father also because where is the love?

It gets very complicated, but it could be very simple. This Adam and Eve syndrome is in your blood, in your DNA. There is a need for security and for sex built into your DNA.

There is a two-fold solution for the battle between the sexes. You must give up getting upset. Upset is your enemy. How do you give up getting upset? Do you deny your emotions? No, you stop trying to heal yourself forever and just give up being upset. Trying to heal everything is simply a pattern. You will not heal everything. Just stop the pattern.

How do you stop trying to heal everything? Every human being has emotions, and your emotions are not reality. Emotions are a part of the coloring of your perceived reality, but they are not reality. Because of your pain, hurt, and resentment in the past, many times at different points in your life you cut yourself off from your emotions or the feelings that really matter to you. Finally, when you have a spiritual awakening all of your emotions come back and you become in love with all of your feelings as though the emotions hold the truth. However, this is a great lie. Your emotions do not hold the truth. They are just another color.

The reason why your emotions feel so good after you have been awakened is that you have been cut off from your emotions for so long you never want to give them up again, nor should you ever give them up again. However, then this perpetual business of trying to fix the wounding begins to happen. You think you must heal everything and everyone. Forget about that. It is a negative pattern of being broken forever that leads to depression, and it is a miserable existence.

How do you get the love you want? First, you must realize that you are not really interested in love. You are interested in power, and that is your problem. You must get interested in love. How do you get interested in love? You recognize that you are interested in power and that what you need is love. Then you get yourself some love and forget about the power trip. Get the love from the center within your still, quiet place. Forget about trying to get love from the places that do not give it to you and start letting it come from the places that give you love. Practice receiving love instead of trying to extract it from a rock.

Instead of fighting with daddy, let love come in and get over your daddy and mommy fights. Get over it. I know you cannot do that easily. I am just saying to do it. That is what you need to do. Get over it and get the love. Stop spiritualizing your wounds and practice love.

Love is a practice. You are full of love, so now practice receiving it. Love is a practice, and you must grow skilled at loving and stop the fight. You must stop getting upset. When you are upset, it is a signal that your ego, your wounded identity is flaring. This is not something to be ashamed about, even though some of the things the ego can do are absolutely shameful, really horrible. The ego can wreck your life and wreck other people's lives with it.

The ego has a tendency to flair when one is upset. Upset does not mean emotional upset in the way that there is shouting or speaking passionately. What upset means is the point where you are imbalanced and you lose consciousness and begin to suffer. That is, the ego flaring or when the ego flares then you become upset. That must be gotten over. That is where you must find peace, and that is a part of mastery. It is a skill that must be developed. It is not about becoming emotionless, but instead recognizing your own ego inflating and deflating.

Only you can notice your ego's position, which is a skill that is developed. You become aware. To recognize your ego flaring is awareness. Consciousness is the ability to express God through you at the moment. That comes from God communion and means you meditate and you draw upon communion with God. However, to get there you must recognize your own upset. Therefore, upset can be a tool to help you discover where you are not you. If you do that enough times, you become a conscious being. For those people who are in man/woman, Adam and Eve battles, that will destroy you unless you have some love.

Sun Bear

Heart is required at the level of entrance into the fourth dimension. The fourth dimension is strongly feminine, and this entrance is one whose time has come for this earth. As the earth moves into the feminine spirit, the doorway to the Great Spirit, where the Goddess is, becomes very, very strong.

It is important to understand the meaning behind the story I am about to share with you because this is the story of the love of the Goddess. It is also the story of how to love in soul mate relationship, and exactly what soul mate relationship is and what God is.

This story is thought to have its origins in Eastern Europe, but it comes from the Great White Brotherhood, the one that the Hopis refer to as the Great White Brothers, which are in fact the Tibetans. This story, generated into the culture of Tibet from extraterrestrial beings, traveled to Europe and to the Inuit, the Indian people of Alaska. Passed onto the people of the Black Feet Nations, it passed on from there downward into the old Anasazi people. From the Anasazi the story passed on to the Hopi Nation, who had a written history that includes this story, in what is now called the southern United States.

☙

There was a very, very poor old man, who had several daughters, and they all lived in a forest. One day a great white bear came to this old man and said, "I want to marry your youngest daughter."

The old man said, "You are a bear. Get out of here. You cannot have my youngest daughter. You cannot have any of my daughters. Get out of here."

The bear replied, "If you let me marry your youngest daughter, I will make you as rich as you are now poor."

When the man heard this he said, "Daughter, daughter, come here." When the daughter came to him the old man said, "Marry this bear and he will make us rich."

The daughter emphatically stated, "I am not going to marry this bear. It is a bear. I am not going to marry."

The bear became very, very sad and his shoulders slumped as he walked off into the forest. As the bear disappeared, the father and his daughter began to talk and the daughter came up with an idea. "Why do not I pretend to be in love with this bear? Maybe I will marry him and, after you get rich, I will find some way to come back home."

The father's response was "That's a great idea."

Some time later the bear returned and begged pleadingly, "Please, let me marry your youngest daughter, and I will make you as rich as you are now poor."

The old man called his daughter forward and the daughter went off deep, deep into the forest with the bear. They walked for miles and miles and hours and hours and days and days. The young woman became ever so tired. When it appeared the young woman was just about to expire she saw before her the most beautiful building unlike anything she had ever seen. It appeared as though it was high in the clouds and yet somehow accessible from the ground upon which she stood.

The young woman sprang to life at seeing such a beautiful structure, the likes of which she had never seen on this earth in all of her experience. As she walked through the cloudy mists toward the structure, a wave of energy came upon her and nearly made her faint. The bear caught her and helped her into the building.

Inside the building, the young woman saw the most beautiful things she had ever seen. There were beautiful treats prepared for her, meats, pastries, cakes, fruits, and vegetable, in the most beautiful array of eating she ever thought was possible. But she was tired and simply grabbed a few things to put in her mouth as the bear said, "Come, let me show you to your room."

The bear and the young woman walked up the stairs in this great structure where she found the most beautiful room she had ever seen. There was a beautiful large bed in the middle of the room filled with goose down feathers. The bear said to her, "Why do not you rest upon this bed and sleep. In the morning we will talk."

The young woman was so amazed and excited and yet so tired that she could barely keep her eyes open. She immediately stumbled to the bed and lay down, falling fast asleep. It was later, in the middle of the night, that she heard her door creaking open and footsteps approaching the direction of her bed. The next thing she heard was the creaking of her bed and a big depression as though someone sat down on the bed. To her surprise, instead of being frightened, the young woman felt greatly at peace. She felt the weight at the end of the bed lie down next to her. It was then that she heard breathing unlike any breathing she had ever heard before, so beautiful and rhythmic and sonorous that she could not help but listen to it as it lull her off into the dream world.

The next morning, as the young woman woke up, there was a knock at the door and she realized it was the bear knocking. Quickly she stole a glance at her bed and it was as though no one had ever been there. The bed was not disturbed at all. The blankets were not disturbed. There was no breathing being next to her. She looked at the bear in the doorway, who was beckoning her to come down to breakfast. "Let us have breakfast together," he said.

The young woman went downstairs to breakfast, and again it was the most wonderful fruits and breads and other foods. The bear and she had a wonderful conversation after which he asked the young woman "Is there anything you need in any way? Is there anything you want for in any way?"

"No," she replied. All of my needs are fulfilled. However, there is one thing. Last night as I slept…"

The bear interrupted her to say, "Shhh. Shhhh. Let us not speak of such things." Therefore, the young woman said nothing more, and the bear and she went about their day.

The night came and the young woman grew tired, falling asleep on her lovely bed. She was filled with wonderful treats and richly supported and complete inside, but again late at night she was awakened by the sound of the creaking of her door. The footsteps again approached the bed followed by the feeling of a big depression at the end of her bed. She was too afraid to look, and at the same time excited and filled with yearning. With fear and excitement filling her, she closed her eyes and felt the huge weight lie down next to her. "Humph. Humph. Humph," the most beautiful sound of breathing she had ever heard, large and strong, yet soft, rhythmic, and comforting. Again, the young woman drifted off into the dream world and slept.

The next day the young woman awakens to the bear knocking at her door and, looking at her bed, sees no depression, nothing whatsoever to indicate that anyone had visited her. It was as though nothing ever happened. When the door opens the bear says, "Why do not you come down for breakfast? I have prepared a beautiful meal for you."

Bewildered the young woman got up. She wondered what was going on, but goes downstairs to breakfast and has the most sumptuous meal she has ever had, even better than the day before. This time there is fruit she has never seen, milk, cereals, and grains. She eats until she cannot eat anymore and yet she was not pained from overeating, just satisfied. The bear queries her, "Is there anything you want for in any way?"

"This is the most beautiful kind of life I could have ever imagined. It is everything I could ever have imagined and more. No, I want for nothing, yet there is something I just have to know. At night there is something…"

"Shhhh. Let us not speak of such things right now."

"Okay." Then the young woman remembered her family. "There is one thing. I miss my family, my father and my sisters."

The bear became very tense and the hair on the back of his neck started to come up. Then he relaxed his shoulders and said, "Alright, we will invite them here. But there is one promise you must make to me and that is you must never come into my room at night and gaze upon me."

The young woman thought to herself that would be easy because she did not want to go into his room at night anyway. "Okay, I will make that promise," she said.

With that promise, the bear went out and gathered the young woman's family. They all trudged their way through the forest to the castle. When they arrived, the young woman's family was amazed at how lavishly she lived, and the bear kept his promise by giving them much money and jewels.

That first night the young woman gathered her sisters in her bedroom and said to them, "I have to tell you something."

Her sisters interrupted her asking, "Dear sister, how can you live like this? We know this place is beautiful, but you are living with this great white bear. How can you stand it?"

The young woman married to the bear answered, "I do not think about that so much because at night there is something very special that happens. Something comes and visits me and it lies down beside me. It is so beautiful and there is such a sweet aroma emanating from this being that is lying next to me. The breathing coming from this being is so sonorous and beautiful that I am ecstatic. I slip off into the dream world and there are the most treasured dreams. But in the morning, when I wake, there is nothing next to me. I do not know what is happening.

The sisters responded, "Oh sister, you known that is the bear."

The young woman married to the bear is astonished and asks, "Are you serious? Can that really be the bear?"

In unison the other sisters reply, "Of course it is the bear." One of the sisters suggested, "Tonight, sneak into the bear's room and watch and see if that bear is leaving his bed and coming to see you."

The married sister thought about that for a moment and then said, "Maybe I will do that."

That night the married sister retired to bed early. She waited until the middle of the night and walked to the room where the bear slept. As she peered into the darkened room, she could not see anything. Carefully she lit the candle she had brought with her and stepped further into the bear's room. As she walked toward the bed, all of a sudden she sees, lying upon a great chair, the largest skin of bear that she has ever seen. Astonished she looked over to the bed and there lay the most beautiful being she had ever seen in her life with the most beautiful smell emanating from his body.

The young woman was so intoxicated that she swooned and could barely keep consciousness. She was so rapt by the smells, the vision and the sounds of his breathing that she was frozen in her position, not noticing the candle wax dripping on the blanket of the being sleeping in the bed. The candle wax dripped, falling on the blanket and awakened the being. He stood up and shouted, "Go from here. Now you have ruined everything."

Deflated the young woman slipped out of the room, off to her room and climbed into bed, finally drifting off into a fitful sleep. When she woke the next day, she was aware that no one came to visit her during the night. She is shocked by this discovery. As she listened for the customary knock on her door, she became aware there was no sound in the great building surrounding her. She did not hear the bear or her family. When she went to investigate, she found the entire castle empty. In her confusion, she did not know what to do. The only thing she knew was that her heart was broken.

Finally, the young woman decided to gather up everything she could carry of her possessions and go searching for the bear. Everywhere she searched, she could not find him. She ventured out into the forest, over hill and dale, avoiding dangerous animals, finding very little food in the cold forest.

Then she ventured upon a very old crotchety woman, who appeared to be knitting something. The young woman approached the old woman and began to cry, "Old woman, you have to help me. I am looking for a great white bear. I have been searching through the forest day and night, through hill and dale, through dangerous animals, with very little food. I have been freezing and I do not know what to do. I am out of my mind with worry.

You see, long ago, this bear came to my father and asked if he could marry me and I said no. The bear said he would make my father rich if I married him. So I thought I would trick the bear and marry him, somehow escaping and getting back to my father after the marriage. Then I went to live with the bear and it was the most beautiful thing I had ever seen. And this being would come to me every night with beautiful smells and sonorous sounds. I was so happy, and would drift into the dream state.

Then my family came to visit me. They said I should go and look upon the bear while he slept to see if it was he who came to my room each night. I broke the rule of the bear and went to his room. I have ruined everything. The bear is gone. He is gone and I do not know where to find him. Old woman, you have to help me."

The old woman said, "Yes, I can help you, but you have to see my older sister. She is deep, deep into the forest and I do not know if you can make it. If you see her, I am certain she can help you."

"Thank you, old woman. I do not care how far your sister is. I will go and find her."

The old woman gave directions, and the beautiful young woman ventured deeper into the forest than she had ever been before. It was further even than she had traveled with the bear to his wonderful castle in the clouds. As she neared the end of her road, certain that she would die before reaching her destination, off in the distance appeared a woman who was dying some knitted material. This old woman was even older than the previous old woman was and she was ugly and spindly. She looked frighteningly scary as though she hardly was alive.

With trepidation, the young beautiful woman approached the haggard old woman. "Hello old woman. I see you are dying knitted material."

In response the ancient woman spit back, "Yes, I am dying this wool for my sister in the forest. Why have you come here?"

"Old woman, your sister sent me here. I am searching for my lover and husband and cannot find him anywhere. He is a great white bear. Have you seen him? You see, one day a bear came to my father and asked if he could marry me. I said no. Then the bear told my father that he would make my father rich. My father and I schemed falsely to get the riches from the bear by marring him, and then I would run away and somehow get back to my father. But when I went off with the bear into the forest to marry him and live with him it was the most beautiful experience I ever had in my life. This wonderful being would come and sleep with me at night.

Then my sisters, who came to visit me, told me it was the bear, even though I could not see it was the bear. Since I did not know it was the bear, I broke one of his rules and tried to find out if the being that visited me at night was the bear.

When I went to see him, the most beautiful being I had ever seen in my life was in his room with the bearskin sitting at the side of the bed on a chair. My lover woke and said I ruined everything. After that everyone disappeared, my father, my sisters, and the bear. They all disappeared, and now I cannot find my husband anywhere. Please old woman, can you help me?"

The decrepit old woman said, "Yes, yes, I can help you, but you will have to see my older sister. She lives deep, deep into the forest, further than anything you have ever known in your entire existence. No one has ever been able to travel that far, except my older sister. Not even I have been able to travel that far, for I have gone to visit my sister, but I died in trying to visit her. But my older sister, who was coming to visit me at the same time, saw me lying dead and found I was not gone too far. With her special spells and potions she brought me back and told me to never try to visit her again. She said she would visit me because she lived much too far for me ever to reach her. So you see, even though I can tell you where she is, I do not think you can make it to her."

The young woman was emphatic. "You do not understand. I will make it. I will not die. I will make it to your sister!"

The old woman gave her directions, and again the young beautiful woman set out over hill and dale in search of her beloved husband. She went deeper into the forest than she had ever known was possible, seeing sights and things she never knew existed. As she walked, she passed between two large trees. Everything seemed as though it became wavy and strange, but she kept walking, even though she felt as though she would faint. She walked a bit further, and everything began to appear the same again as she continued to walk deeper and deeper and deeper into the forest.

At one point, the young woman stumbled and fell. She was out of food, frostbitten, frozen, and starving. It was at this point she saw off in the distance an old, old, old, older than life itself, ugly woman with big eyes popping out of her skull, skin drawn against her bones, the ugliest, skinniest, must wretched looking fangs grown long and coming out of her mouth, and dirt and scum covering her, and with the most horrible stench coming from her that was imaginable. But the young woman, thinking only of her husband, approached the disgusting creature. "Old woman, may I talk with you?"

"How did you get here? How did you find your way here?"

"Your sister sent me," said the young beautiful woman, looking closely at this woman before her who did not even look like a human being. In fact, she looked like some kind of human lizard monster or something. Nevertheless, the young woman persisted, first having to know one thing. "Your sister sent me here, but where am I?"

"You are east of the sun and west of the moon."

The young beautiful woman began to relay her story to the old, old woman. "Old hag, your sister sent me here, your younger sister, because I have been searching for years and years and years to find this great white bear, who is my husband. He came to visit my father and me one day and asked if he could marry me, the youngest daughter. I said no. Then the bear offered my father all of this money if I would marry him.

My father and I then plotted to trick the bear out of his money. But the plot turned out to be crazy, because when I married the bear a being would visit me when I was sleeping every night in the bear's castle. This being was so beautiful that I fell in love with him.

My sisters came to visit me and told me that the being who visited me every night, which I never saw, but only felt and smelled, was the great white bear. I thought it could not possibly be the great white bear, but snuck into his room at night to look upon him, which broke his rules. As I went to look upon him, my candle tallow fell upon his blanket and woke him.

I ruined everything and he disappeared. My family disappeared. I have been looking for him for years and years and years. Your sister sent me here and said you could help me. Can you please, please help me find my love, who means more to me than anything I have ever known?"

The old withered hag said, "Look over there."

The young beautiful woman looked where the old hag was pointing with her crooked lizard finger, and there by a table was a huge white bear. The young woman turned to the old hag and asked, "Is there something wrong with him?"

"Heh, heh, heh, my, you are young! He is dead."

The young woman fainted straight away.

When she woke from her faint, everything was changed. Along a wall, the young woman saw woman after woman after woman after woman all lined up in chairs. One woman was taking a blanket and trying to wash tallow out of it, all the while saying, "I will show you how to get tallow out of the blanket." She washed and washed and scrubbed and scrubbed on the scrub board, but the tallow would not come out.

The next woman said, "I will show you how to wash tallow out of a blanket." This woman scrubbed and scrubbed and scrubbed and could not get the tallow out of the blanket. Then each woman after her in the long line of women tried to get the tallow out of the blanket without success.

When there was no one left in the line of women, the young beautiful woman walked over to the blanket, picked it up ever so gently and put it in the water. She then lifted the blanket out of the water with the greatest of care and love, and then slowly pushed it back down into the water. Low and behold, the tallow came out of the blanket.

From behind the wall appeared a being, the most beautiful being the young woman had ever seen. Beautiful smells started to come from him and wonderful colors and beautiful, beautiful expression of his heart. Overwhelmed, the young woman nearly died. Yet she remained conscious as the beautiful being said to her, "Yes, I am alive. I have come back to you. Even though you did not recognize what you had when you first saw me, I have come back to you. My name is love."

The End

☙

Think about this story in terms of soul mate first, perhaps the kind of soul mate that you had learned never to search for because the search had become hopeless. Then think of this story in terms of Great Spirit and feel how this story and Great Spirit may be very close to each other. Maybe the great white bear has already visited you and you must find him again, past the pattern of your jaded expectations. How far are you willing to go?

Beloved souls, you must be weary of popular culture because even though this story is like a fantasy, how many would say this kind of thing is obsession, codependent or unrealistic? Nevertheless, what about eternal truth that goes deeper than anything you could have ever imagined? What about when you find yourself in such a position that you are the one pulled further than anything you have ever been through before? Have you ever let yourself go through that? Have you ever shielded yourself from experiencing like that?

Let me tell you a few qualities of soul mate that are very, very close to entering the doorway into the fourth dimension and the God love, because one thing begets the other thing. Consider for a moment what a soul mate would look like who appeared when your eyes were closed. This is not someone you saw, but someone you felt so that your eyes did not distract you. That being would have insight, loyalty, and devotion. They would care about their own independent being and be very concerned with you and your feelings. With your eyes closed, you would feel kindness there.

Another thing you would notice in this soul mate is the ability to learn, because those who cannot learn will also become intolerant. In addition, can they be like you if they want to be? Can they overlook certain faults? Can you overlook certain faults? Often these faults come in the form of endearing qualities that later become annoying habits. Can they be more at peace than you can? That does not mean they have to be a bum, but can they back off now and then? Can they add to your life and make it bigger rather than making it smaller?

All of these qualities are also the doorway to the Great Spirit. There are other qualities to Great Spirit, but they are very hard to see. They are qualities that are easier to see in partnership or in a loved one. If you want to open the door to the Great Spirit and if you want to open the door to deeper or new love, you must be aware of these things. Great Spirit can come into you and clear you of your blindness and inner obstacles that have kept you from the sacred name of love.

Read the story again, not trying to understand any of its deeper meaning. If deeper meanings come, let them. However, some things in the story do not need to be explained or understood. They are just integrated into your inherent self-knowledge so that if you just read again, the God-consciousness, the love consciousness within you is awakened.

That is the purpose of this story. It holds a certain key that can help. It is about sensuality. There are two kinds of eroticism, you might say. One kind is very physically sexual and leads into a higher dimension. The other kind is in the higher dimension and leads to something very sensual or physical. This story is about sensuality, about intimacy, and about passion. Therein lays the key to awakening and spiritual union.

Merlin

Sex is a very powerful instinct because it is not just sex, but is the ultimate survival. How could your bodies, which are busy surviving, have gotten here without sex? Therefore, your physiological foundation is the by-product of sexual involvement deeply rooted in the race and its urge for survival. How powerful is that?

Sun Bear

The longing of a woman is completely to face anything in order to penetrate obstacles and be intimate with the one she loves, no matter what. This is also the need of the man, but the man does not believe it is possible. The heart of a woman, the searcher for the lover, always feels that it is going to be too late. Her search is hopeless. Yet, in the end, love is reawakened despite everything. This is the heart of a woman. Women need to know this and men need to know this.

Because women have become disempowered down through the ages and are just now coming into their power, there is a confusing thing occurring that has something to do with this idea of codependence. I use the term codependence in describing a woman being subservient to the misguided rule and domineering nature of the man and thereby being used and abused without regard for her value. This has occurred historically. However, because it has occurred historically, it has caused the birth of a wrong perception. This wrong perception is that a woman must be like a man in the world when a woman and a man must in fact be very different from one another in the world to have love and in order to know the Great Spirit.

Do not buy into the current psychology of codependence that says a woman must be like a man. While the idea of codependence is helpful in regard to women who make themselves victims and disempowered and need to stop making themselves available for that, it is terribly confusing in terms of who a woman is. A woman is a being of extreme giving, which can bring the spirit of man to life, in fact, can bring the spirit of anyone to life.

Why would gender make such a difference? Why would a genetic inclination or predisposition make that much difference? It just does. For example, do you know how close human beings are in genetic composition to the fly? I believe there is only one genetic component that is different between a human being and a fly, yet one is a little tiny fly and the other is a great big human being. They are very different from each other.

What I am saying is gender makes a great deal of difference. The mind, the intellect cannot appreciate what is necessary in order to be at peace with regard to this gender matter, this love matter and this God matter. The intellect cannot adequately address these things. It is a matter of another dimension of consciousness needed to address these matters.

In terms of capacity to actualize equivalent brilliance and superior expression of talent, there is no difference at that level between women and men. However, at the level of sensuality, intimacy, romance, and endurance, women are very much more powerful in general than men. Men can kill the mightiest dragon for the right woman, which would be impossible for any other being to kill. However, men can do it only one time. Women however can endure eternity at any moment. This indeed is a superior strength, not an equivalent strength, but indeed a superior strength.

At the level of the intellect, there are many differences, but they are all equivalencies. The differences are compatible and inter-functional, inter-relational and can create a comprehensive whole, impossible by the male psychology and the female psychology as it is presently demonstrated in your world. However, at the level of romance and intimacy what is necessary as a mortal being to cross the infinite, women primarily hold the key to this more than men do. It is not an equivalency.

The struggle for women to be equivalent to men, because they have been disempowered, is very misleading. It is like a short-changed target that most women who try can easily manage, by they way. It is not easy, but it is within their capacity to manage if they try. In the end however, they will be short-changed because there is a different outcome available to both women and men. If men and women seek to fulfill their genetic composition, they will find not only what is their expertise and excellence, but also they will be able to find their humanity in a way they have never been able to discover before.

The era presently unfolding in your world is in fact about this discovery of gender excellence. Moreover, if you are a human being in the flesh, you must pass the test of gender relations, whether in the form of male and female or two females or two males or multiple partners. You cannot get God-consciousness unless you first resolve the seemingly competitive agencies and agendas of the gender relationship of man and woman. It does not matter what sex you are by your physical organism. What matters is your genetic construct, because at the level of your genetic construct is an expression of your spiritual psyche, so it has got to be resolved.

It is possible for an individual to have all components of both gender relations such that they can manifest a God-conscious relationship without a partner. That is extremely rare because human beings come here into physicality in part specifically to address this gender dissimilarity and resolve it. It is an essential need to embrace what would otherwise be conflicts at the dimensions that are higher above this. Therefore, it is important to learn how to see Great Spirit within the opposite gender relation.

It is important to note that different sexual organs do not mean opposite gender expressions. It is very possible to have same gender organs and find compatible opposite gender, male/female gender, in the same physiological sex. That does occur and there is a very important reason for that at the level of one's genetics.

Merlin

Some of you may have found yourselves in the position of being taken advantage of in one way or another. Please understand that you have a role in it even though you may not know how. You may or may not have caused it, but you have a role. Your role is to be one who assumes responsibility for your own well-being, even though you may not have created the conditions that caused your lack of well-being.

Let us say that you have been sexually molested as a child and it has had terrible consequences throughout your older life. What put you in that position? There are some who would quite deftly say that you have been the molester in another life and it has come back to you. It really does not work like that, not at all. It works more like this. Life prospers in primitive conditions toward more enlightened conditions depending upon the ability and the willingness to be adaptable within that context.

In other words, even though you might have been unjustifiably preyed upon as a child, it falls to you to take responsibility in that circumstance to correct the conditions of your life and psyche. That may seem unfair to you, but that is by your own context of what is fair and unfair. What you may not know is that you have also been provided the ability to address that context. That is why you have intelligence and that is why you have Guides. The universe works in many ways that you know and do not yet know, and you will be guided to that which knows.

Sun Bear

Absolutely there is not just one soul mate for each person. If you are in Florida, there is a soul mate for you in Florida. If you are in China, there is a soul mate for you in China. If you are in India, there is a soul mate for you in India. There are soul mates everywhere for you. This is not because soul mates proliferate, even though certain aspects of God do proliferate. Instead, it is like this. If you are a person who needs to eat, God does not make one apple on a tree for you. God gives you tons of apples on a tree, so many that you cannot even eat them all yourself. That is what Great Spirit likes. However, you must give up certain conception, demands, and needs such that you are properly receptive and attentive to the qualities of soul mate.

Soul mate really is a being who is beautiful, mysterious, perfect and opportune, unexpected, unusual and inconsiderable in some sense. That being is around you right now. The question really is, if you have not found that being, are you ready for that right now or are you looking for something else?

Azlo

We consider sensual education to be imperative, particularly for children, because it is strongly linked to the awakening of your mind. Your senses are the key to the mind, and you should not deprive yourself of sensual fulfillment. Surround yourself with music, art, meditation, beautiful colors and smells, as well as all that is beautiful to the touch. You will inspire your own genius if your environment is a sensual one. Teach your children this. You will be in harmony with infinity if you are as this. Think of it like this, to be sensual is to have your environment give you pleasure.

Remember sexual education also. The usefulness of your sexual organs may be important, but it is not as important as the awareness of your sensual being. Teaching only the utilitarian purpose of your sexual organs is foolish. Do not teach your children that their sexual organs are bad or wrong, and do not teach them to be ashamed of their bodies. Teach them to relish and enjoy their bodies.

For those who cannot understand, think of it like this. Would you teach your children that music is only for marching or writing or for paying your bills? Thanks to artists who make there art for pleasure you have begun to expand your understanding far beyond utilitarian purposes. Teach this also when you teach about your bodies. They are for pleasure and not merely utilitarian. Teach your children this without shame that they may blossom fully.

Also, teach your children to respect the freedom, rights, and peace of others. Their pleasure and joy must exist within the boundaries of certain freedom and respect for others. However, life without pleasure is like an uncultivated garden.

Sun Bear

At some point, life requires a consciousness that is something like love. Consciousness itself is a consequence of love. Let us take as an example, have you ever fallen completely in love, like head over heals totally in love, not infatuation that passes, but deeply in love? You begin to feel like the whole world is full of life. Everything takes on new meaning. You begin to understand why things have happened the way they have happened, and you begin to be thankful for all that has happened to bring you to this point. All of a sudden, everything in your life seems to fall into place because you feel a consciousness like love.

If you have no love in your consciousness, what happens? You do not feel like you understand anything. The whole world feels as though it is closing down on you. Nothing seems to have any meaning, and you feel separate from everything. Have you ever noticed that?

Consciousness requires love. In other words, the more goodness that is in your consciousness, the more alive you will be. When there is an absence of goodness or love from your consciousness, the less alive you will be. Life expresses differently for different life forms, but in order for you to have more life you must have more consciousness that is like love. To have more love, you must have consciousness of more life.

If you started to let in more life force, would you become more vital? Would you become stronger? Yes, you would. However, every place inside of you that has an obstacle to being alive or being more like love will come up inside of you. This can bring up incredible terror just because more life force came into you. You might not expect that, but that is what happens. If you can continue onward, your dreams will start to change and your energy will start to change as your life rearranges itself.

Azlo

Pregnancy, childbearing, and the way you treat women on this planet is really very painful and difficult. You do not need to do it this way.

Philos

Eventually, you will increasingly see a number of other ways to create human life other than by the organic birth of a child produced through sexual intercourse of men and women. Childbearing through a woman was designed intentionally to sufficiently slow the process of the development of humanity. Humanity was growing too quickly in intelligence without maturity and would have folded in upon itself in self-destruction if not for the current design of childbearing.

The life forms of this world, and throughout the entire universe, are slowed by the sort of pregnancy and birth that you currently experience. Life forms that grow in the greatest numbers do so much in the way cancer cells grow, by splitting off from one another. No intercourse is necessary in this process.

Cloning and other forms of life unfolding will grow popular over the decades to come. Within a few centuries, birth through the woman's body will entirely be phased out of life in human civilization. This will lead to human beings no longer having a need for their current sexual organs.

Sexual pleasure is truly a function of the brain organ more than any other organ. This being so, increasingly in your lifetime you will see the stimulation of pleasure centers in the brain that is safely accomplished, also stimulating creativity and intelligence. Over centuries, the by-product of pleasure stimulation not resulting in the birthing of new life forms will allow humankind to become increasingly creative, productive, and expressive in all ways, including scientifically. The increase in these areas will be without the inhibitions that are created by the current levels of struggle. Human beings will no longer give their lives for each other in order to support the current structure of familial organization.

Likewise, your society will see the increasing number of lovers of child development become the caretakers of your children and not necessarily those who bring forth the life of the child. The favored form of love within humanity at this point to bear and remain close to families, despite all of its good intention, creates separation.

Merlin

In your relationship, it may be that your partner is unable to call forth sufficient love to respect and honor your position. Maybe they cannot give you what you desire from them in relationship. Perhaps it even looks to you as though what you want from your partner really is not that much. What you are looking for may be commonly expected in relationship, but it is not there in your relationship. It might be that the person with whom you are in relationship cannot call forth the part of themselves that would respond to your need for love.

For both of you your efforts in the relationship may feel like trying to draw water from a rock. However, you do not know that is what you are trying to do because the expectation is to get water, which you know is there. You might be full of that water and willing to give it, so you cannot imagine why the other person, whose very soul you have seen and whom you love, will not bring forth their water when they promised their love to you. You may even wonder if something is wrong with them or with you. However, that consciousness cannot yet be brought to bear, and there is nothing you can control to cause it to be brought to bear. Either your partner or you are just not ready.

You may not be as ready as you think in that you cannot see that your partner is not ready. If you were as ready as you thought, you would have been able to notice a partner capable of giving you what you sought. Therefore, that consciousness does not exist in you. Your hope and belief in the soul self that you have seen in the other person exists and you are expectant. Yet there is something that prevents you from being wise enough to see that they are not available, thus letting your partner go.

Letting go is the part of love you are able to do, which allows you to move into the next dimension, a fourth dimension of consciousness. Fourth-dimensional consciousness is less self-centered and more concerned with a duty to a higher truth.

Philos

In your world, emotion is a powerful catalyst toward many right and wrong directions. It is not the emotion itself that is problematic, but the lack of consciousness or awareness. The emotion is identified with as though it is self, and yet it is just an emotion. It is important to understand the distinction because your emotions can be powerful teachers. Even though what you feel is not the entire reality, there are clues to insights in your feelings that are important.

When you feel romantic love you tend to feel powerful emotions, and your need is for love. Even the most close-minded people, whether they like it or not, still need love. Therefore, love is often the savior for those who would otherwise know no greater reality. Love grabs at the emotional level, even though it is not an emotion, and stimulates the body. Because of this, one becomes open, through the emotional body, to something greater.

Love with any person, father, mother, child, intimate partner, art form or for anything whatsoever charges the emotional body and is the key to the unseen. The love you feel powerfully in your emotional body, even if it causes you pain, and oftentimes love can cause pain, can be the key to the Infinite. It causes many people to open in ways they never intended to open. In this way, their spirit is awakened.

Sun Bear

It may cause you to wonder why what you call great men marry women who are strong-willed and who nag them, telling them what to do. It is because these women hold wisdom. The woman that a great man marries will keep him alive. And if she is a good woman, she also will love him.

Sun Bear, Chief Great White Eagle, Two Trees

Unconditional love is power. It is the ability to be outside of demand and to be accepting. Unconditional love is a difficult state for most human beings.

Cassandra

People who grow through love are sometimes attached to each other in healthy ways, and sometimes attached in unhealthy ways. It is sometimes hard to know the difference. Nevertheless, in the end, one of the things that love demands is that somebody, who truly loves another person in the highest form of love, can support another in being able to move on. That is the highest form of love, helping another to move on. Not everyone is expected to receive the highest form of love, for that demands a great deal of true understanding of all forms of love. Sometimes people are simply not at that point. Therefore, sometimes one simply makes decisions that they feel and know to be right for themselves while simply trying to be as loving as they can. That will not always draw the result they want from another person though.

Sun Bear

There is much misunderstanding about men and women in this land, and many things about sexuality you must understand in order to have successful relationships. To begin to understand we must go back a number of years to when your people arrived in this country.

When the newcomers came to this land, what you now call the United States, we liked them. They liked us for the most part. We ran into conflicts a little down the road because of propriety to the land and because of our different ways.

The newcomers to this land came here because they strongly wanted to practice their many different religions. We liked that.

Most of the people, who came at that time, came from certain Christian lands. They came with their strong religions, but when they lost their religion, they got a new religion here.

However, what happened was there was one particular sect of the Christian religion called the Puritans, who ended up with dominance in the way that the Christian religions evolved here in this country. Not all of the Christian religions were the same, and the differences caused some struggles. However, the influence of the Puritans in the north and the east ended up the influence that very much affected the kind of Christianity that eventually was practiced here.

We did not have a problem with that. What we had a problem with was the affect it had on sexual relations between men and women. Puritanism caused much confusion in the gender consciousness of men and women all throughout our society. The problem became that men and women did not any longer know what they wanted. In trying to figure this out some went back to the old ways and some tried the new ways. This caused much more confusion because men and women need each other. This still has to get sorted out and sorted out quickly.

There is some place further to go with relationships in this world, and there must be a good foundation of gender consciousness before relationships can get to the next place. It is important because you are losing your partnerships. Your women are losing their men and your men are losing themselves.

Cassandra

What people do not really understand about love is that love does not mean you must be together. That is an illusion that comes from fear for safety and security, and it keeps people from their ultimate freedom. Ultimate freedom is a form of love where all that comes from an entity is support and all that entities receives is support, so they are always free. They first must learn how to create forms of love like that, and there is a great deal of schooling that the human spirit must undergo to get to it. At this time, the planet is not anywhere near to that ultimate love.

Sun Bear, Chief Great White Eagle, Two Trees

Let us say you are looking for a partner and you meet someone. The first thing people usually wonder is whether or not the person they meet is 'the one'. Why do people get so confused about this? It is because there are so many things on their plate that they do not have a clear sense of who they are and who they are not. Thus, they are asking the wrong question. The questions they should be asking are why do I not clearly know what I want one way or another, and how can I know?

How can a person be open to knowing the truth when their needs demand and compel them to shape things according to their needs? The first thing they need to do is get less needy. One gets less needy, less desperate by being clear about who they are and who they are not. Mostly you can be clear about who you are rather than who you are not. Then when something does not fall into a category that is a reflection of who you are or who you are not there is a little inner voice that says, "Wait and see," unless you are too needy. Therefore, you have to get out of that needy state that is demanding.

Sun Bear

Within you is an inner demand to live. Yet in your culture your body, sex, and emotions are all tied up as something you are supposed to disregard. At the same time, you are also taught to pay a lot of attention to your body, sex, and emotions while you are supposed to be disregarding it. This leads to shame, which is like self-hatred that goes very deep. It is a profound guilt, like self-punishment, that comes after you feel guilty. When you feel guilty, you have to sentence yourself and the sentence is shame.

Cassandra

Energetic initiations are experiences whereby you have an opening of certain energy centers or chakras to some new level that affects the spirit, mind, and body. When you have an initiation of the heart chakra, you will feel exalted love for life and for everyone.

When there is an initiation at the uppermost chakra, you are in a state of spiritual bliss, as though the whole world is seen as a perfect expression of divinity where everything works. You understand that you are in perfection and are one with God. Everywhere you look all you see is God. This can continue for a while and means that this door has opened.

An initiation of the chakra in the third eye leads you to understand the reasons for everything. You open also to having lucid dreams. These dreams happen spontaneously, not because you try to make them happen. At this level of initiation, reason and rational become very important and that is when the door opens.

When you have an energy initiation in the throat chakra you have a desire to speak or express everything that is going on within you. That means you are no longer one who keeps your words within, but allows whatever is going on in your consciousness to be expressed.

Energy initiation at the sex chakra feels like an urge to bond with and touch all of nature, all people. It feels like strength in your physical body. You may have a desire to make sexual or physical communications with as many people as possible.

The chakra just below the solar plexus, when initiation occurs, will feel like a great sense of personal will and staying power with the sense that you are able to follow anything upon which your mind sets itself. In the period of time of an opening at this level you may find yourself needing or wanting to control all of the situations around you to make things happen. On a psychic level, this energy further empowers whatever you visualize to come to pass. It enables you to follow through with anything that would otherwise be difficult and empowers and inspires others to be able to find their way also.

The root chakra, which is just underneath the sexual chakra, when open feels like a sense of balance in your life, flow, and harmony. There is a sense of everything in its place and a place for everything.

All of the chakras need to be opened, but are not opened in everyone. Some people are born into this life with experiences that primarily have been focused around one or a few energy centers to the point they are born with gifts because these energy centers are still active. In other words the energy that they are as a soul places itself in their new body, focused around whatever energy centers were their previous talents. The soul does this because that is what it is used to and what it is experienced in doing.

There is no system by which the chakras open. Sometimes the centers can be opened, and then they may close up for some reason. You also may wonder why it is, after many, many incarnations, that your energy centers have not been initiated or opened. It is because in each life you are born, if you are an older soul, with all of your energy centers open in a sense. Some centers may be a little more open than others may, but in the struggle to survive from youth to adulthood and all the experiences that you go through people can begin to close down their openness as a result of hurt along the way. This deprives them of the power they need to express their mastery.

When the energy centers open, it is impossible not to notice them. This does not mean that later, when the experience subsides, that the centers are closed. It is just like a dam breaking. First, there is a flood and then there is a flow. Mastery is when all the energies are open at the same time. When you find yourself in mastery, it will be because you, in effect, have opened all of your energy centers.

Sun Bear, Great Bear, Sam Strong Body & Chief Great White Eagle

You are very fortunate if you never meet your twin soul. If you are in the United States, your twin soul ought to be in China. It is better never to meet your twin soul.

Some people speak of one's soul mate as a twin soul, meaning perfect match. We speak of twin soul in a way that never, ever could be a soul mate. Twin souls can get along with each other, but they can never be soul mates. A twin soul is like two beings that exist in a split condition, one spirit split into only two spirits. Their particles are organized in such a way as when they incarnate they are like two sides of one coin with one side being a head and one being a tail. They are twins with the head facing one way and the tail facing the other way, never the twain shall meet. If twin souls somehow turn around where the head and tail face each other, they will repel each other. They cannot stand each other and cannot be in each other's presence. They are in fact the same, but they are meant to go in opposite directions.

In this sense of twin soul, you will usually instantly recognize your twin. They will be someone so much like you that you cannot stand them, even if they are developed spiritually. It may be the karma of twin souls to function in business and work together or to be in the same family. In fact, there are many elements of twin souls between children and parents. However, heaven help the relationship where you get a full twin as a child or a twin soul as a parent. That is very difficult to do. It also is possible to have sexual relations with a twin soul, and it might be very hot and fiery, but you may not get along with a twin soul at all outside of the bedroom.

As for soul aspects, there are many forms of soul aspects. Soul mates are soul aspects of one kind because they have aspects of each other's particles. Soul twins are aspects that are completely opposite of each other, even though they are from the same singular entity at one time. Soul brothers or soul siblings, soul sisters, soul parents, soul teachers are all kinds of soul aspect relationships.

It is possible to have a romantic and sexual relationship with anyone. Nevertheless, if you are talking about intimacy in a long-term partnership, it needs to be at best a soul mate or some other complimentary form of union that satisfies your needs as a being.

Souls can combine many ways in long-term relationships without being soul mates. For example, many people are together permanently who are not in love with each other, but deeply love each other because of what they go through over time. Maybe a man and a woman are from a very small community. They both feel a need to get out of that small community. The man has a sense of adventure. The woman has a need for growth. They get married and have children right away and then find out they do not really belong together, but they are committed to the children and they do not know what else to do. Love was not the reason they got together, which would have been the right reason. Their need to survive and escape their conditions was what brought them together, and they can develop love, respect, and appreciation from working and living together and raising a family together. They have a desire to be with each other because they have shared so much together.

This kind of relationship can be 'till death do us part', if the death age was thirty-six or something like that. However, since people now live into their seventies, eighties, and nineties, oftentimes such people split up around their thirties and go on to a second marriage or even a third. Because of the basis upon which people get together, some people can have three marriages in one lifetime based on convenience for the stage of life in which they are and their needs. That is one way someone can have successful relationship that is not to the end of life, because a soul needs to do its business.

Because souls who get together like this have aspects in common, the particles of one soul needs to experience adventure and the other soul needs to escape a repressed condition, they both serve each other's spiritual agenda. They get together and help each other fulfill the other's spiritual agenda. That is a kind of soul aspect relationship and can be a good one, but it is not necessarily based on coming together in love. It is based on coming together because there are harmonious needs in common for survival of the soul and psyche of both individuals. That is an example of soul aspect love and relationship.

Sun Bear

There is something we refer to as the Adam and Eve syndrome, which is like a metaphor. In this syndrome women use sex and men use security to get their needs met from each other. Men learn to manipulate women in exchange for their protection and comfort. Women learn to manipulate the sexual needs of men. This is not who people are, yet there is an instinct to use what you have to get what you want. Not only is it instinctual, but it is passed on in the culture.

If you do not wish to participate in the Adam and Eve syndrome, there is tremendous pressure on you culturally. There is a pull deep inside to act as those around you are acting, otherwise a false identity or persona is created to cover up other things that are going on deep inside of you. All kinds of misunderstandings flow forward from this because you are covering up instinctual demands and have very little power to exert the higher truth.

A man may say that he wants love and can give love, but does not really care what the woman looks like. Then, when in relationship, that same man may stop having sex with his partner because she has put on fifty pounds or maybe the man wants children and his partner cannot have any children. Perhaps she makes demands for things he does not have the money to buy for her. The man then feels angry or inadequate and he may not want to feel that way. In reaction to feelings of anger or inadequacy, a man may start looking for a woman who does not care so much about money, which is a reaction to a pattern and not a solution. Alternatively, he may look for a woman with a better libido, a reaction to the last thing he found.

How can one focus on a spiritual journey when the whole matter of human instinctual demands, including the sexual nature, are complicating the mind and emotions unbeknownst to you? Therefore, the first thing you must do is open your eyes and see what is truly running your show.

Merlin

Many are those who have been betrayed by a lover and not been able to get over it. Even though some are enlightened, they still cannot easily get over that sort of thing, which is difficult and troublesome. The answer is for you to throw yourself into service, and it will help. That is why you do service, because it helps.

Sun Bear

A woman wants to give herself completely and know that it is safe to do so. She wants to be received by a man.

Merlin

At certain points along the journey you are either going to be alone or one partner is going to be open and the other hardly not even there until a time comes when both partners are open. The reason is that at the level of relationships where most people desire them, they are for a very functional animal purpose. People want relationships to have babies, to make their lives easier, or to create a sense of security. Simply put, that is why people have relationships, even though they think it is for the purpose of love.

At the higher level, relationship can ultimately lead to love. However, when it comes down to love in relationships most people in relationship will turn around and say that love is not enough. They want someone with money in the bank account and someone who can manage their affairs or one wants a baby or marriage and the other does not. Many things come into play when people are in relationship.

The greater purpose of relationship, at the level most people want them, is survival. You are raised as part of a world culture and so you have similar desires for security, sexuality, children, and mutual support, making each other's lives easier. These are the needs human beings have in common. Therefore, even when you want to have a higher relationship, survival is the primary basis upon which you are drawn to relationship.

When you try to draw in a higher relationship that is free of the survival needs, you find out how much those things matter to you. Moreover, if you think you have drawn someone into relationship that is not at your level, then how did you draw in someone like that? It is because you had the same desires in you that other person had and the same needs. That is how you ended up together. It is also possible that you started out with the same needs and one of you grew more than the other grew, which does happen more than it does not happen. However, this is only important if you must stand on the truth of what you know and accept the consequences, which all must do sooner or later.

Sometimes you find out that it is completely acceptable to have a relationship because it addresses certain needs. It is up to you to hold a higher love, the best way that is possible, while your other survival needs are being met. It is as simple as that. However, when you are ready to have a relationship matched at the level of your mastery, it is not about needs anymore. It is about something else.

If you are looking for a soul mate, I promise you, you had better be ready to go beyond your needs. You also had better know what your needs are because if you are a soul mate, this is not a needs-based relationship. It means you must be prepared to know a love greater than your needs, even when your needs are not addressed, because it is not about a relationship at the level of your needs. It is about love, the transmission of love freely back and forth, which may have very little to do with your needs or demands.

If you leave someone on the basis of your mutually incompatible needs, it is because your demands are not met and you have to find someone who will meet your needs or your demands. That is what demands are, and you are allowed to have them. You need your demands, and so you should not try to get past them when you need them. However, you must know your demands for what they are. They are your needs. They are not bad, but are a part of every human being. When you are ready for something different, you can take that step.

Imhotep

Of all that is important, the most important thing to focus upon is the power of love. Make love your primary focus. It does not matter what you think love is or is not. What matters is that thoughts and inclinations toward love are cultivated.

Love is a power that at some point makes most entities uncomfortable, for love is a power that must be embraced in one's entire being, and it brings the force of life. To that extent that one allows love to be present in their being and in their body, to that extent can one then radiate existence, health, and aliveness. To the extent that one does not know the power of love, to that extent does one experience a diminishment of life forces. Therefore, it is by merely focusing upon the principle of what love is that one then embraces the power of life. This power is something that is always with you, and it makes your mind clear and opens your destiny. The power that is love must be the focus that guides all forms of spirituality.

Many wish to know what disciplines will open the doors of the various planes, chakras, and mystical experiences. Techniques or disciples do not matter, but what more easily opens the doors is that which one is focused upon with love in one's heart. Whatever one's practice, if one will first focus upon the center that is the heart, one will begin to feel a relaxing of the physical body and a gentleness of spirit. In a short time, that gentleness of spirit will expand into great feelings of love, warmth, and safety. Any discipline practiced within the presence of that power is practiced within the presence of love.

Sun Bear

The place where Spirit connects with the physical body is like an orgasmic state. It may appear the body is where the physical experience of orgasm takes place. However, in fact, orgasm takes place beyond the body in consciousness, in a place of great sensitivity, receptivity and openness, between the realm of dream and the realm of touch.

Azlo

The conception of a child is very important. A child should only be conceived in love, and the highest possible love at that. If a child is not conceived in love, consider not having the child. Children are much too precious to bring into the world other than in love and in proper care. They are you heritage. You must guard your children, love them, and protect them.

Sun Bear

Consciousness exists in particles that collect and band together to form an entity that then divides and subdivides into many beings. Over many incarnations, human beings combine and recombine with so many particles of consciousness from one another that essentially it becomes one person looking out of a thousand different eyes. Most people are many of the same particles, but organized in consciousness where one or two or a group of particles is dominant in one human being while another group of particles is dominant in another human being. This leads to the appearance that human beings are different from one another. Ultimately, the purpose is for all particles of consciousness to find some form of complimentary harmony and to grow and evolve. Part of the growth for a human being definitely lies in the ways human beings connect in loving relationships of all kinds.

Sun Bear, Great Bear, Sam Strong Body & Chief Great White Eagle

Soul mates relationships are far from perfect. They are very powerful and quite intense at times because there are soul particles that need to learn better integration. The very fact that the souls are in cosmic union nearly all of the time brings up tremendous psychological and emotional issues at the level of the physical body. Therefore, it can be said that the love that exists as a result of spiritual intimacy brings up everything unlike love that exists in the psyche of those two human beings who are soul mates so those things can be cleared away.

At a certain point in time, if two people who are soul mates are not committed to each other and committed to being together, they will part. However, when they part they will still feel connected to each other for their whole life, even if they never again see each other. That is why they tend to return again and again to this dimension. That is why soul mate is the best type of relationship for a long-term relationship, but of course, it is not the only type of relationship.

There are soul brother and soul sister relationships that can become a soul mate relationship, because theoretically all souls must enter into some form of harmonious union without a fight, anywhere from a tolerance to an acceptance, but a strong connection. Soul mates must originate at some point, so it is possible for any form of soul combination to evolve into a soul mate relationship, even in the course of one life, but usually it is over the course of many lifetimes.

There are also relationships that are conflicting and karmic. Sometimes people are drawn together in an unhealthy way and may not even be aware of it. For example, let us say a woman was repeatedly sexually molested a child, maybe ritually molested as part of a terrible negative religious ritual. This is more common outside of the United States, but also goes on inside of the United States. Let us say that person, when they grow up, escapes what goes on within their family unit. Obviously, because this went on within their family, there may be many unresolved issues because generally, as children, everybody needs the safety and security of their parents, but not everybody gets it. Everybody needs the love of his or her parents, but not everybody gets it.

Subliminally such a person, molested as a child, may look for something that is missing from their childhood because they may recognize this psychically in another person. They may have a nose for this if another person has been involved with some sort of similar or complimentary negativity. They are used to this kind of person and they easily recognize the symptoms. They can sniff them out. When they meet another person like that, without even knowing that person may have a similar or complimentary history, they are inexorably pulled together and have a terrible relationship. The level at which they got together is just too undeveloped, too sick.

Many times very negative things come out of those relationships, but they can also initially be extremely irresistible and compelling. Oftentimes such persons have a pattern of getting into the wrong relationships over and over again, and that should not be mistaken for soul mate relationship. That is a sort of relationship based upon the familiarity of negative history and unconscious negative patterns, but can be every bit as compelling as a soul mate relationship.

Sun Bear

You may not be aware just how much your body has to do with your spirit. You may also not be aware just how much your thinking has to do with your body and your emotions. Even statements such as it is important to love yourself, to love your body, are taken casually. Those who feel they understand the significance of this may not be aware of how important these statements truly are. Statements such as your body is the temple of your spirit may be understood to one degree or another, but sometimes the very same statement to some people means that it is a sacrilege to, for example, eat the wrong things or to expose the self sexually to the body.

There are entire religions that would have some people believe that you are somehow more holy if you are non-sexual. That is in fact true, to the extent that there are significant practices that are important that involve no sexuality. However, these practices are not for everyone, just as it is not for everyone to be a monk, and not for everyone to be married. There are certain things for certain people at various points along their spiritual journey. Moreover, the very same thing that is holy and sacred for one person may be very profane to another person, depending upon where the person is and what is necessary for them on their spiritual path. There is not really a single prescription for the spiritual journey for every human being, except that every human being, at some point, in some incarnation, will go through everything every other human being will go through.

Sun Bear, Great Bear, Sam Strong Body & Chief Great White Eagle

Everybody is challenged very deeply at some point by some aspect or another in his or her partner. However, someone who really loves you will come to love you no matter what. People must be harmonious at the spiritual level, and then they can have many differences at the practical level.

On the contrary, if people have many things in common at the practical level, but they are different spiritually that will never work. For example, people have a common interest of the same music and they have the same financial approach to life and many other things in harmony, but one of them is Jewish and another one is born again Christian and they are strongly in their cultural and religious views. This will never work no matter how much they have in common. However, if they have the same spiritual context, then even if they have many differences at the practical level, it is going to work out one way or the other.

The point of all love is to become unconditional and unlimited. It does not start out that away, but must eventually become unconditional and unlimited in nature. Marriage relationships are not unconditional and unlimited love. Marriage relationships start out with many conditions and within certain limitations. However, sooner or later they may have to expand in order for there to be lasting marriage.

All kinds of relationships move toward becoming unconditional and unlimited love even though almost all relationships start out on conditions such as looks, things in common, common goals, and other things of that sort. Sooner or later, if there is real love there, and this is usually the love that is a symptom of a soul mate relationship, everything else is gradually let go and people appreciate and love each other.

This kind of love brings up outrageous fears in people because nobody wants to be rejected. Everybody wants to be accepted for exactly where they are right now. One wants to be felt deep down inside. One wants to be known. One wants to be loved and appreciated for who they are right now. However, in order to do that people build up many barriers and many safety conditions before they let themselves have relationships. That does not work for old souls though. It may work with younger souls, but it does not work with older souls. Older souls are more responsive to things externally that they have in common with another. By externally I also mean the other person's persona, their spiritual attitudes, and if the other person can fit their entire agenda, and then they wonder if something is missing.

The key is that one may be in a position in the karmic continuum where it is up to them to learn to trust and follow their heart, even if some aspects of one's outer condition and conditioning does not match what one thinks it should. In addition, with a soul mate you always know because words will often follow like, "I do not understand you, but I sure do love you." That comes with the soul mate and is a hint that a person is a soul mate.

Sun Bear

Very few people in your culture long stay spiritually connected when it comes to the level of sex. Quickly a spiritual connection at the level of sex can become instead a physical connection or a combination of many intertwined psycho-emotional issues.

It is important to understand that the physical body is an expression of the spiritual body. You may look at your body and not like it and wonder how it could be an expression of your spirit, but that really is a temporary emotional condition. However, when a person becomes sexual or seeks to become sexual, they need to know their body. It requires a person having a feeling about who they are and about their body beyond an immediate emotional reaction to the state of affairs of their body. Either you like your body or you do not. It is either too skinny or too fat, too much hip, not enough hip, breasts too big, breasts too small, too much pot belly, not enough six pack. All of this is temporary feelings, temporary conditions about which you may have some association and feeling. However, this has nothing to do with the knowing of your body in the overall context of self.

When we speak of including your body in knowing and loving self, it is not dependent upon your immediate psychic or emotional reaction to the state of affairs of your body. It is a greater context of knowing about who you are and where you are in the scheme of things. This awareness is something that one must bring to the body and therefore bring to the sexual experience.

Sometimes this is done when a person is engaged in a loving or sexual experience with someone else, but it is very difficult for most people to maintain this awareness over time in the sexual experience. Usually the awareness degenerates to some other place than the awareness of who they are in the scheme of things. The less frequently that one has this kind of connection to themselves, very often one loses the ability to remain aware, loses the practice of what it even means to be holistic in one's approach to the body, lovemaking, and spiritual development. If one spiritually approaches sex, meaning the consciousness and maintenance of awareness of self, then it is an entirely different matter than approaching it physically and psycho-emotionally.

Sun Bear, Great Bear, Sam Strong Body & Chief Great White Eagle

You can be with a soul mate and he or she utterly and totally may reject you after first completely accepting you, leaving you feeling betrayed. You may not understand what happened and can find no explanation for the rejection. They may just disappear, cut off without as much as a word. That is because love brings up everything unlike itself to be resolved. Many people do not expect this, and when it happens, they are just out of here. However, the way they are soul mates is that, even though it hurts terribly and feels completely disrespectful with you never wanting to be in that position again, you still somehow feel this incredible connection with that person at the level of soul. Moreover, even if you do not want it and try to ignore it, that connection still exists. That is proof of a soul mate. You can be assured that soul mates are not perfect relationships, but they are beautiful relationships. When people are committed to each other, these are the most beautiful kinds of relationships.

Sun Bear

As part of having happiness in partnership, you must either get to the place where you like your body or let a partner help you like and love your body.

Sun Bear, Great Bear, Sam Strong Body & Chief Great White Eagle

You must be in the habit of bringing your authentic self to your partner. To bring your authentic self to your partner, you must be aware that a lot of things pass for the self that are not really the self. Maybe a person has some need for which they are trying to compensate as a result of not getting what they needed when they were young. Maybe they never felt understood or loved enough or given to enough by their parents. In a relationship, they want their partner to understand that need that previously was not addressed. However, that need is not the self.

You are welcome to try to get your needs that previously were not addressed met by your partner in relationship. That is fine, because you should be able to ask for your needs to be met. However, what are you in the practice of giving that is truly the authentic self? To learn this you must first be with yourself.

Giving of the authentic self must first be practiced. It is like a healer or someone who channels Spirit. There is an opportunity for a great deal of energy to move through a person who is able truly to give of the self. It is the same energy that sometimes moves through people in meditation. If one remains sensitive to the energies moving through them, they may feel all kinds of things going on within themselves. That energy is called the self, the authentic.

Most of the time a person does not need to have all of the self present in order to function in the world. All that is needed is a certain amount of understanding about how to function, and then a person can function fairly well in the world. The authentic self can remain disconnected and a person can still easily function. Nevertheless, whatever amount of consciousness comes through a person to be used in the world, it is that which is usually thought of as self.

A person becomes identified with self as all of the level of energy coming through them with all of the related thoughts and emotions, but that is just a pattern, not the self. What about the self that is so great that a person does not even call it self, what if that were brought to bear in partnership? In other words, do not confuse the authentic self with some sort of an act or a performance.

Sun Bear

When sexual energy moves upward in the human body it tends to bring enlightenment. However, it is not normal for sexual energy to move upward in the human body. Normally the sexual energy flows downward toward the genitals. It may start as a mental or higher energy of the mind, but ends up in the genitalia, and is an energy drain. Nevertheless, when the energy is spiritual and it enlightens, it can often start lower and tends to end in the up energy.

For most people sexual stimulation begins in the mind. However, when it is a spiritually enlightening experience, even if it begins in the mind, it tends to anchor very quickly in the body, and then flow upward into the mind and spirit. It will go there again and again, and will eventually result in an expanded consciousness.

Expanded consciousness does not necessarily mean that when the energy flows down, people go to sleep and when it flows up, they remain alert. What expanded consciousness means is that when the energy flows downward people do not know what to do with each other after the sexual experience. Whether they fall asleep or remain awake, they sort of do not know what to do. They become uncomfortable, nervous, disconnected, and end up in some other place than in a union.

In a spiritual union, the energy ends up in harmony, rapport, love, and communion. Whether they are awake for discussion, fall asleep, or continue onward physically there is a complete oneness and comfort with each other that enlightens. No matter what the process has been prior to it, breakthroughs, discomfort, comfort, it ends in a higher experience.

Sun Bear, Great Bear, Sam Strong Body & Chief Great White Eagle

At the most expansive level of your being you can love everyone because everyone is one with everything, and you are one with everything. However, when we speak of partnering, partnerships are very conditional. Not everyone wants to be with a partner forever. It is like this, everything has a beginning and everything must end. Love does not have to end, but partnerships change over time. Human beings tend to want to find a lifetime partner because they do not want to have to go in and out of relationships too many times during the course of their life. It can be very heartrending to undergo parting and starting over, but does not need to be nor should it be. Practically however, it is very difficult for human beings to go in and out of intimate relationships.

In the past, it was actually easier to go in and out of relationships because relationships were based on survival needs. People came together to produce families so that they could live in tribal groups, social groups, cultural groups, and nations. Partnering in these ways supported the growth of the community and the family. Now, as things have evolved, people want to get together, not on the basis of need and survival alone, but want to get together on the basis of love. That makes things interesting because love ultimately is unconditional, but relationships and partnerships have conditions.

Most people love their mother and father, but you may not want to spend the rest of your life with your mother and father. You may love your brother or your sister, but you might not want to live the rest of your life with your brother or sister. Maybe you do, but maybe you do not. You can love your daughter or your son, but maybe you do no want to spend the rest of your life living with your daughter or son, or you might.

Everyone has certain desires, wants, wishes, needs, and expectations and everyone makes partnerships on the basis of mutual fulfillment of what is important to them, their more important values. Ultimately, true love will creep into these kinds of relationships and cause a person to break down the barriers of their conditions and circumstances and move gradually toward unconditional love.

People have such a hard time in relationships trying to figure out who they are, what they want, and whom they want because what brings them together is a combination of their needs, attraction, and love, but their needs and preferences change. Therefore, coming together on the basis of needs and preferences is, at best, a temporary situation.

If you are going to remain with a person in relationship, you must expand the ways and the whys and wherefores by which you come together in relationship. In so doing, you are exposed to an opportunity to grow toward unconditional and unlimited love. Unlimited means you must find things like forgiveness, which is not necessarily the thing you may want to find.

People get hurt in relationships from time to time and feelings get hurt. In order to forgive you must expand, let go, broaden the context of your love, having a bigger and grander sort of love, if you wish to remain together with your partner. It is not necessary to remain together in order to love, however people tend to want to remain together. Staying together requires that they seek to find ways to open their being to embrace what will require them to find more love, greater love, and love that has less and less conditions with lots of forgiveness. If not, they will not be able to stay together for very long.

Sometimes people can love each other more easily if they are not together. This sometimes is discovered after they have married and had children. These partners just cannot seem to work things out and cannot even stand each other sometimes. However, they come together for the purpose of the children and they work things out. Even if they get divorced, they will try to work things out, often for the sake of the children. In so doing, many times people find what they loved in their partner in the first place as they cooperate to raise the children, even if they remarry different people. There is a certain kind of expansive love that can exist between people who are separated or divorced, even if they are remarried and in other relationships with other family units. Sometimes in creating space, people in fact find ways to love each other.

It is not necessary for soul mates to be together all of the time. It may be desirable and may be extremely important at some times, and for long periods of time, for soul mates to be together. However, soul mates are those whose souls are always in some sort of union, no matter where they are in the universe. Even if they are physically apart, in a way, soul mates are really still together. The question of soul mates is a very expansive thing. The question of love is a very expansive thing. But the matter of relationships and getting along with each other and sharing life with each other, this is another matter altogether.

Sun Bear pp. 97 -102

Made in the USA
Lexington, KY
05 January 2010